FIELD
INSTRUCTION

FIELD
INSTRUCTION

A GUIDE FOR SOCIAL WORK STUDENTS

THIRD EDITION

David Royse
Surjit Singh Dhooper
Elizabeth Lewis Rompf

University of Kentucky, Lexington

 LONGMAN

An imprint of Addison Wesley Longman, Inc.

New York • Reading, Massachusetts • Menlo Park, California • Harlow, England
Don Mills, Ontario • Sydney • Mexico City • Madrid • Amsterdam

Editor-in-Chief: Priscilla McGeehon
Acquisitions Editor: Janice E. Wiggins
Marketing Manager: Wendy Albert
Project Coordination/Text Design/Electronic Page Makeup: WestWords Inc.
Cover Design/Manager: Nancy Danahy
Illustrator: Chris Rosenthal
Full Service Production Manager: Eric Jorgensen
Print Buyer: Denise Sandler
Printer and Binder: The Maple-Vail Book Manufacturing Group
Cover Printer: The Lehigh Press, Inc.

For permission to use copyrighted material, grateful acknowledgment is made to the copyright holders on pp. 4, 19, 58, 119, which are hereby made part of this copyright page.

Library of Congress Cataloging-in-Publication Data

Royse, David D. (David Daniel)
    Field Instruction : a guide for social work students / David
Royse, Surjit Singh Dhooper, Elizabeth Lewis Rompf.—3rd ed.
        p.   cm.
    Includes bibliographical references and index.
    ISBN 0-8013-3044-0 (pbk.)
    1. Social service—Field work.   I. Dhooper, Surjit Singh.
II. Rompf, Elizabeth Lewis.   III. Title.
HV11.R67   1998
361.3'2—dc21   98-9686
                                                               CIP

ISBN 0-8013-3044-0

1 2 3 4 5 6 7 8 9 10–MA–01 00 99 98

Contents

Preface

If you are about to begin your first practicum, this book was written for you. It is a "survival manual" or "consumer's manual" designed for students. Although we had undergraduates primarily in mind, the material is also applicable for graduate students— especially those who come into social work from some other discipline.

Most students find the practicum to be a valuable experience that confirms they have made the right career choice. Still, being placed in an unfamiliar agency and being assigned real clients may make some students a little anxious and unsure of themselves. Even confident students have questions prior to and during their field experiences. By offering practical advice for some commonly raised questions, we hope to reduce your anxiety so that you can maximize your learning and development as a social work professional.

Field Instruction: A Guide For Students can be used by educators in two ways: (1) as a supplement to practicum manuals or other materials often provided by social work programs to their students; (2) as a stand-alone text designed to prepare students before or as they begin their field experience. You'll find ample "case examples" and questions crafted to stimulate class discussion and reflective thinking. In addition, every chapter contains suggestions for activities or assignments.

We have tried to be comprehensive but succinct while staying to our mission—this guide is not intended to replace practice texts used in social work foundation courses. For some important topics, the discussion is designed to be a quick refresher of what students probably already know. This guide also addresses questions (e.g., "What is Malpractice?" "How Do I Handle Sexual Harassment?") not likely discussed in theory courses.

We have attempted to provide the type of advice that students will find useful even though social work programs vary greatly in the way they are structured and administered.

Few programs supply students ahead of time with information about the problems most commonly encountered in the field. Undoubtedly, some material provided in this book may be conveyed orally or via handouts to students enrolled in practicum courses. However, we all know that handouts can be lost—often when they are most needed—and that we don't always hear all that we should. Many students will find this guide to be a quick and accessible reference they will want to add to their private libraries. Its convenient size makes it easy to carry along in a backpack or bookbag.

We hope that in some small way our book will make for a better field instruction experience for all of those involved—students, instructors, clients, and supervisors. Field instruction is a significant part of social work education and we feel that it is always unfortunate when a practicum is viewed simply as "volunteer" activity. Apart from the tremendous learning and refinement of skills afforded in a well-planned practicum, students have enormous responsibilities whenever they serve clients as representatives of social service agencies and institutions of higher learning.

Several new topics have been addressed in this edition, including: New sections on Managed care, new and revised material on diversity, expanded material on safety issues, and a new essay on handling stress. You will also find an expanded chapter on legal and ethical concerns, and new examples and illustrations in students' voices. Also, we have updated references—adding new ones and dropping old ones. Once again, please notice that we have used interchangeably the terms field instruction, field work, field experience, practicum, and internship. Similarly, persons supervising students in the field can be known as agency supervisors, field supervisors, intern supervisors, or field instructors. Of these terms, we use *agency supervisors* and *field instructors* interchangeably. Finally, faculty supervisors, field coordinators, seminar instructors, faculty advisers, faculty consultants, or faculty field liaisons are always referred to as *faculty field liaisons*.

Thanks to our reviewers: Cynthia Leonard Bishop, Meredith College, Joan Merdinger, San Jose State College, Gary Shaffer, Univ. of North Carolina at Chapel Hill, Jim Stafford, Univ. of Mississippi, and Barbara Wickell, Univ. of Illinois at Chicago. Special thanks to Holly Riffe, Ph.D. for writing the new section on managed care.

Should you have any suggestions for new topics, or would like to supply a humorous or instructive illustration for us to incorporate in the next edition, please contact us.

David Royse (droyse@pop.uky.edu)
Surjit Dhooper (dhooper@pop.uky.edu)

Chapter **1**

Field Instruction and the Social Work Curriculum

Overview

This introductory chapter provides the historical and current context for understanding the requirement of field instruction in social work programs. It also begins to answer questions about student preparation, supervision, and the coordination of field instruction within the larger educational program.

Why Do Social Work Students Have Field Instruction?

As professionals in the making, social work students attend classes to learn practice principles, values and ethical behaviors, a body of specialized knowledge, and the scientific basis for practice. In field instruction, students apply what they have been learning in the classroom to real situations. Thus, the preparation to become a social work professional is composed of formal learning as well as practical experience—sometimes known as field instruction, field placement, field work, practicum, or internship. Such training experiences are not unique to social work but are common to most of the helping professions.

A career in social work requires many abilities. Social workers must have competence in relating to individuals, small groups, organizations, and communities; in assessing needs and problems; and in planning and intervening appropriately. Social workers have to be skilled in carrying out various helping roles such as advocate, broker, educator, group leader, mediator, clinician, community planner and organizer, administrator, and so forth. While students may not be able to acquire expertise in each of these roles during a single practicum, placement in an agency allows them the opportunity to observe other professionals and to learn from their actions. Students can learn from any of the staff around them—all play a role in helping students to become more proficient.

Students not only acquire practical experience from the field, they are also socialized into the professional subculture. There are two important aspects of this socialization: acceptance of individuals into a professional group where common expectations are held of all members, and the development of a professional self-concept consistent with role models. During field instruction, encounters with clients, colleagues, and the professional community help to educate and indoctrinate students into the culture, norms, and values of social work. Field instruction assists students in making the transition from passive learners to active professionals.

Field instruction is one of the nine areas constituting the social work professional foundation content required in both undergraduate and graduate social work programs (Commission of Accreditation, Council on Social Work Education, 1994). It is, however, of singular importance. It is in the field that material covered in the foundation courses on human behavior, social policies, research, and social work practice gets a real-life examination outside the classroom. The practicum is particularly helpful in providing students with experiential learning in the other foundation context areas: social work values and ethics, diversity, promotion of social and economic justice, and populations-at-risk.

Field instruction is a valuable part of the social work curriculum because it allows students to test whether social work is the best career for them. The choice of a career is a major decision, and not everyone is suited to be a social worker. Because students are closely supervised and evaluated, faculty field liaisons can help students identify their strengths and weaknesses and determine whether or not social work is the best choice for them. Occasionally, faculty field liaisons must recommend that students address personal issues before entering their field placements.

Case Example

John has changed college majors four times in the past three years. He entered as an English literature major, then changed to accounting. In his sophomore year he tried both geography and Russian. After one year of Russian, he dropped out of school to "get his act together." He worked as a bartender and jokes about how easily drunks can be shortchanged and their drinks watered down. When a DUI conviction caused him to lose his driver's license, John took a couple of social work courses and did well in them although several of your friends say they have smelled alcohol on his breath during class. Last week John was fired from his job for stealing from his employer. He claims the charges are not true and plans to go to school full time next semester to become a social worker because, he says, "It's easy work—all you have to do is talk."

Questions
1. Is John ready to become a social worker?
2. What questions could you ask to help John examine his motivations for becoming a social worker?
3. Why, in your mind, should a person choose the career of social work?
4. What characteristics make a good social worker? A poor one?

What is the Role of the Faculty Field Liaison?

The primary job of the faculty field liaison is to see that students' practicum experiences are educational. Rosenblum and Raphael (1983) describe specific faculty field liaison's duties as (1) facilitating field teaching and students' learning, (2) overseeing educational opportunities offered by the agency, monitoring students' progress, and fostering an interchange between school and agency, and (3) evaluating field instructors' efforts and students' achievements. Faria, Brownstein, and Smith (1988) identify ten liaison responsibilities, which they divide into six roles and four functions. The faculty field liaison functions are:

- *Placement*—selects field agencies and field instructors, and matches them with students.
- *Linkage*—interprets school policies, procedures, and expectations of field agencies, and assesses the fit between school curriculum and educational experiences provided by the agency.
- *Administration*—ensures completion of placement forms (e.g., students' evaluation of agencies, field instructors, and faculty field liaisons).
- *Evaluation*—evaluates students, field instructors, and agencies; assigns students grades; and makes recommendations for continued use of agencies and field instructors. (More on the evaluation of students in Chapters 2 and 4).

In the performance of their functions, you should see faculty liaisons in the following roles:

- *Adviser*—provides assistance to students in planning for practicum.
- *Monitor*—assesses agencies, field instructors, and students' learning experiences.
- *Consultant*—assists field instructors in developing supervisory skills and providing course outlines and other materials.
- *Teacher*—assists students with the integration of course work and practicum, and serves as a role model to students.
- *Mediator*—assists in resolving problems between students and field instructors or other agency personnel.
- *Advocate*—provides relevant information to academic review committees (when necessary) to evaluate students' field and academic performance.

In many programs, faculty field liaisons conduct seminars to provide students with a regular occasion to share their learning and to ask for information or assistance when difficult problems arise. In addition, students may be expected to submit weekly logs of their field experiences and plan individual conferences with their faculty field liaisons. These seminars and conferences provide opportunities for faculty to get to know students, to be able to guide them when necessary, and to help with integrating theory and practice.

What is the History of Field Instruction in Social Work?

Field instruction has always been a major part of social work training. Its history goes back to the days of the Charity Organization Societies in the last quarter of the nineteenth century, when students learned social work by apprenticeship. Through "applied philanthropy" students obtained firsthand knowledge of poverty and adverse social

Printed with the permission of Chris Rosenthal.

conditions. With this *apprenticeship model,* training emphasized "doing" and deriving knowledge from that activity. By the end of the nineteenth century, social work was moving away from the apprenticeship model.

The first training school for social work was a summer program that opened in 1898 at the New York City Charity Organization Society. In 1904, the society established the New York School of Philanthropy, which offered an eight-month instructional program. Mary Richmond, an early social work practitioner, teacher, and theoretician, argued that although many learned by doing, this type of learning must be supplemented by theory. She called for a permanent group of instructors to direct the work of students, to give them theory and practice together (George, 1982).

At the 1915 National Conference of Charities and Corrections, presenters emphasized the value of an educationally based field-practice experience, with schools of social work having control over students' learning assignments. This idea put schools in the position of exercising authority over the selection of agencies for field training and thus control over the quality of social work practice to which students were exposed.

Early in social work education a pattern was established whereby students spent roughly half of their academic time in field settings selected by the school of social work with the school overseeing the students' experiences (Austin, 1986). This paradigm was made possible by the networking that emerged from the early organizational efforts of social work educators. For instance, in 1919 the Organization of the Association of Training Schools for Professional Social Work was chartered by 17 programs. By 1923, 13 of the original 17 schools were associated with universities or colleges at the postbaccalaureate level. The American Association of Schools of Social Work, in its curriculum standards of 1932, formally recognized field instruction as an essential part of social work education (Mesbur, 1991).

During the first part of this century, psychoanalytic theory dominated social work education. This influence tended to focus the attention of students and social work educators on a client's personality rather than on the social environment. Accordingly, social casework as learned in the practicum emphasized helping the individual more than bringing about social justice or social reform (Sikkema, 1966).

The depression of the 1930s and the enactment of the Social Security Act of 1935 brought about major changes in the country's provision of social services and need for social workers. This marked the beginning of the government's acceptance of at least some responsibility for all vulnerable groups. Until then, local government authorities had grudgingly provided for the bare survival of deserving poor. This act authorized federal grants to states for statewide public assistance programs (Lourie, 1971). Subsequent amendments to this act created several social welfare programs that have affected many dimensions of people's lives.

From about 1940 until 1960, an *academic approach* dominated social work education. This approach emphasized students' cognitive development and knowledge-directed practice. Professors expected students to deduce practice approaches from classroom learning and translate theories into functional behaviors in the field (Tolson & Kopp, 1988).

Educational standards for field instruction were refined in the 1940s and the 1950s, and field work became known as field instruction. A subcommittee on field work for the American Association of Schools of Social Work took the position in 1940 and 1941 that field teaching was just as important as classroom teaching and demanded equally qualified teachers and definite criteria for the selection of field agencies (Reynolds, 1965).

In 1952 the Council on Social Work Education was established and began creating standards for institutions granting degrees in social work. These standards required a clear plan for the organization, implementation, and evaluation of both in-class work and the field practicum.

The *articulated approach* characterized the third phase in the history of social work field instruction (from about 1960 to the present). This method integrates features from both experiential and academic approaches. It is concerned with a planned relationship between cognitive and experiential learning and requires that both class and field learning be developed with learning objectives that foster their integration. It does not demand that students be inductive or deductive learners but expects that knowledge development and practice will be kept close enough together in time to minimize these differences in learning style (Jenkins & Sheafor, 1982).

The 1982 Curriculum Policy Statement further emphasized academic control of educational experiences in field instruction as distinct from an apprenticeship model of training (Austin, 1986).

While there are differences among social work programs in how field instruction is conceptualized and administered, each accredited program must meet standards set by the Council on Social Work Education (CSWE). More importantly, there is virtually no disagreement among social work educators about the educational emphasis that should be placed on field instruction and the necessity of its close integration with theoretical and knowledge-based instructional courses.

What Are the Current Standards for Field Instruction?

The Council on Social Work Education requires that undergraduate programs provide each student with a minimum of 400 hours of field instruction. Graduate programs must arrange a minimum of 900 hours. The Council mandates that every program "establish standards for field practicum settings that define their social work services and practices, field instructor assignments and activities, and student learning expectations and responsibilities" (Commission on Accreditation, CSWE, 1994, pp. 103 & 142). The Council further stipulates that the practicum be a clearly designed educational experience and that social work programs have articulated standards for selecting agencies for the practicum, for selecting field instructors (agency supervisors), and for evaluating student learning in the practicum.

Your particular program may require more hours of field instruction than the minimum expected by the Council. This works to your advantage because more experience gives you a greater chance to refine your skills and to develop expertise.

Case Example

Betty thinks that the requirement of 400 hours in an unpaid field placement is too much—mainly because it takes away from time she could be on the tennis court. Tennis is easily the main interest in her life and always the major topic in any conversation she starts. Betty has the potential to become a professional tennis player and make more money than she ever would as a social worker, but wants the BSW to fall back on.

Her supervisor's schedule does not overlap with every hour Betty is supposed to be in the agency. Halfway through the semester Betty confides in you that she has slipped out two or more hours early each day her supervisor wasn't in, and also lied about the number of hours that she was supposed to be in the library doing a search for literature.

Questions

1. What is your reaction to Betty's confiding in you?
2. Does Betty have the characteristics that make a good social worker?
3. Does 400 hours of field experience seem an excessive amount of time to prepare you to be a social worker?

Are There Different Types of Field Placement?

Social work programs can organize the required field instruction in different ways as long as degree programs are educationally directed, coordinated, monitored, and meet the requirements of the Council on Social Work Education. The most common types of field placements are block and concurrent. Under the *block* placement arrangement, a student is placed in a social service agency with an approved learning plan for a block of time—a whole academic term, two full terms, or a summer term. The students devote full time (four or five days per week) to experiential learning from assignments in the agency. Under a *modified block model* students participate in field instruction in a social service agency four days each week while the fifth day is reserved for taking courses.

Under the *concurrent* placement, the students' time is divided between classroom learning and field work experiences. (Typically, students are expected to be in the agency for two or three days per week and to take classes for two or three days.) The exact proportion of time devoted to each set of learning experiences varies, depending on the type of academic term, the number of academic credits, and whether or not the students are undergraduates or first- or second-year graduate students.

Social work programs across the country have mixed and matched these two types of placements to create models of field instruction. Sometimes first-year graduate students do a *concurrent placement* (two days per week for two semesters) and second-year students complete a block placement (for 15 weeks at five days per week). Larger schools may offer as many as three models of field practicum for students: the *standard model*—two years of concurrent placements for 28 weeks each year at three days (21 hours) per week; the *extended model*—two years of concurrent placement for 42 weeks each year at two days (14 hours) per week; and the *reduced field instruction model*—one year of placement for 33 weeks at four days (28 hours) per week. Educationally, all of these approaches are considered sound, although students who work and go to school may have preferences for one model over another.

How Are Students Prepared for Field Instruction?

At the undergraduate level, social work programs must prepare students for beginning *generalist* social work practice with individuals, families, small groups, organizations, and communities. To reach this objective, most programs follow a three-step graduated approach. At step 1, students enroll in an introductory course in social work and may need to make application to the program.

Step 2 is the completion of basic core courses—social work practice, human behavior and the social environment, social welfare policy and services, and social work research. Step 3 is the placement of students in their field practicum. Faculty field liaisons assign students to social welfare agencies so they can acquire new skills and further refine their existing skills. In many programs, the practicum is scheduled for the senior year.

As an undergraduate student you can expect to spend between one and a half to two days a week in the field agency during a typical semester if you have a two-semester field sequence. The Council on Social Work Education requires a minimum of 400 clock-hours in the field although it is not unusual for programs to require a few more hours than this.

How Are Students in Field Placement Supervised?

In most programs, students are placed in a public service agency under the day-to-day supervision of a field instructor who is a social worker employed by the agency. It is the responsibility of the field instructor to provide students with opportunities for contact with various client systems and to oversee students' performance with assigned tasks. Field instructors are considered members of the extended teaching staff of the school and may be granted faculty privileges such as the use of the university library facilities or discounts at the university bookstore.

Field instructors should be well aware of the social work program's philosophy, the content and sequence of courses, and the expected level of student performance. Often there are special training sessions for new field instructors—this ensures that assignments given to students are consistent with students' abilities and the program's expectations. In addition to the supervision students receive from field instructors, social work programs usually assign faculty members as advisers to students and as liaisons between the agency and the school.

Social work programs vary considerably from school to school (and sometimes even within a school) in the level of student monitoring that field liaisons do. Some faculty field liaisons will meet with their students weekly, but others may meet at the beginning, at the midpoint, and at the end of the term. Other faculty field liaisons may meet only for an evaluation at the end of the term. Some faculty will monitor students' progress by requiring written or oral assignments (e.g., case presentations, planned observations, or interviews); others do not. Even though your field instructor may be asked for a recommendation on the grade you earned in your practicum, the assignment of the grade is most often the responsibility of the faculty field liaison.

How Are Classroom Learning and Field Instruction Integrated?

The very nature of field instruction fosters integration with classroom learning—particularly when students meet regularly to discuss what they have been learning. Students often are amazed at how much knowledge they have acquired when taking turns to describe their interesting or problematic cases.

Social work programs have also employed a variety of approaches to nurture integration of theoretical content and field instruction. Some have developed close relationships with agencies and may provide consultation or occasional in-service training to the staff in host agencies. Field instructors may also serve on advisory boards to provide feedback on the social work program's field education component. Whenever the faculty and the staff of field agencies meet and discuss mutual concerns, opportunities arise to explore ways to integrate students' field experiences with classroom learning.

Efforts to achieve integration can also be more purposive, as when agency field instructors supervising students for the first time are required to attend seminars on field instruction. These sessions facilitate the integration of field and classroom experiences as field instructors are given access to syllabi, course outlines, bibliographies, curriculum statements, field manuals, newsletters, and other relevant documents.

Most social work programs place the major responsibility for the integration of classroom learning and field instruction on the faculty field liaison. As discussed earlier, the faculty field liaison may use methods such as field seminars, commenting on students' logs, or holding conferences with students to increase the integration of classroom and field experiences.

The student's role, too, should be recognized. Students can enrich their learning by sharing relevant information that they have come across, and by making a point to bring into the classroom their interesting field experiences, discussions, cases, and learning from their agencies. Equally valuable is the habit of reflecting on what is being learned in the field. Students should periodically ask themselves questions such as: what knowledge, skills, or values am I learning in field? How workable are the theories that I have been learning? How do situations encountered with real clients mesh with what I have been learning in class? Such reflection, practiced from time to time, not only helps students integrate classroom content and field education, but also promotes students' growth as active, responsible, self-directed learners.

Do Students with Undergraduate Field Instruction Get Credit When They Work Toward a Master's Degree in Social Work?

Yes. Most Master of Social Work (MSW) programs allow applicants with Bachelor of Social Work (BSW) degrees from schools accredited by the Council on Social Work Education to apply for *advanced standing* status. If given this status, students are usually granted a waiver allowing them to receive credit for undergraduate field experience. Depending upon the program, students with BSWs from accredited programs may be allowed to waive one or two semesters of coursework.

The CSWE's Curriculum Policy Statement for Master's Degree Programs states that duplication and redundancy of content mastered at the baccalaureate level must be avoided in master's programs. BSW graduates entering MSW programs should not repeat professional foundation content mastered in the BSW program. "In order to verify mastery and to prevent unproductive repetition, master's programs must develop explicit policies and procedures relevant to admission, course waivers, substitutions, exemptions, or advanced placement" (Commission on Accreditation, CSSW, 1994, p. 138).

Although the basic qualification for advanced standing is graduation from an accredited undergraduate social work program, most programs also insist that applicants earn at least a "B" average in their social work courses. A written examination covering foundation course material may be required, as well as a personal interview.

Is It Possible for a Student to Have a Field Placement Where He or She is Also Employed?

The answer is a qualified yes. Although this option is not routinely available to undergraduates, programs do occasionally allow students to be placed in the same agencies where they are employed. Because certain conditions must be met, not all employment situations qualify as field sites. Students are to be employed in agencies meeting all field instruction and other program standards and expectations. Other requirements often include: having responsibilities different from those customarily performed, having a MSW supervisor different from the regular supervisor, and receiving permission from the employing agency for release from paid duties during regular business hours in order to be a student.

The relevant CSWE guidelines read as follows:

> If the student is also employed in the agency where the field practicum takes place, the availability of release time for course and field instruction should be ensured. Student assignments and field practicum supervision should differ from those associated with the student's employment. It should also be

demonstrated that there is no diminution of the program's established require-ments in class and field practicum and the field instruction is educationally focused rather than solely centered on agency services (Commission on Accreditation, CSWE, 1994, p. 129).

The best rationale for requesting a practicum in the agency where one is employed is the availability of unique educational experiences—exposure to a clientele or inter-vention not available at any other agency. Some agencies also encourage their employees to "cross-train" so that they have a pool of better qualified and experienced staff on which to draw. These agencies may be willing to provide release time for student-employees to learn different skills within the agency. The concern that most faculty field liaisons have with allowing students to have a practicum with an employer is that it may be difficult for the students to be viewed as "learners" by the student-employee's col-leagues. Because of their knowledge of the agency and its programs, these students may be given so much responsibility that they are unable to read, study, or reflect on their new practice experiences. As a result, these students may be so busy (especially if not given release time) that they are unable to differentiate between hours spent as a regu-lar employee and time spent as a student intern.

In our experience, large agencies (such as hospitals) provide the best models for sit-uations where students could be both employees and students. For instance, Sue could be a hospital social worker assigned full time to the maternity unit. If a practicum with-in the psychiatric unit could be worked out, she would have different responsibilities and supervision. When working in the maternity unit, it would be clear that Sue was func-tioning as an employee, and when working in the psychiatric unit, Sue would be func-tioning in the student role.

Ideas for Enriching the Practicum Experience

1. Interview a student who has just completed a practicum and ask this person to describe the most valuable lesson that he or she learned in the practicum.
2. How long has the social work program been provided at your college or univer-sity? What local agencies were involved and supportive at its start? What were practicums like when the program first started, and how have they changed? Ask the social work librarian or reference librarian to help you find material to answer these questions.
3. Find the Yellow Pages of your telephone directory where social service agencies are listed. Can you identify public and private agencies? How many of the agen-cies have names that make it difficult to know the population or type of problem with which they work? How many of the agencies are you familiar with? How many are you encountering for the first time?
4. Take a moment to reflect on the type of cases or community problems that you will encounter during your practicum. Get on the internet and see if you can find any useful resource material.
5. How many fields of service can you identify where social workers are typically employed? List as many as you can and then check this list against the areas of

service identified in *Social Work Abstracts,* published by the National Association of Social Workers in Washington, D.C.

6. What are your particular strengths, abilities, and talents? Make a list of these and any skills or competencies you hope to develop during your social work practicum.

References

Austin, D. M. (1986). *A history of social work education.* Austin, TX: University of Texas at Austin, School of Social Work.

Commission on Accreditation, Council on Social Work Education (1994). *Handbook of Accreditation Standards and Procedures* (4th ed.). Alexandria, VA: Council on Social Work Education.

Faria, G., Brownstein, C., & Smith, H. Y. (1988). A survey of field instructors' perceptions of the liaison role. *Journal of Social Service Education, 24*(2), 135–144.

George, A. (1982). A history of social work field instruction: Apprenticeship to instruction. In B. W. Sheafor & L. E. Jenkins (Eds.), *Quality field instruction in social work.* White Plains, NY: Longman.

Jenkins, L. E., & Sheafor, B. W. (1982). An overview of social work field instruction. In B. W. Sheafor & L. E. Jenkins (Eds.), *Quality field instruction in social work.* White Plains, NY: Longman.

Lourie, N. V. (1971). State administration of public assistance. In *Encyclopedia of social work,* 16th edition (pp. 1046–1056). New York: National Association of Social Workers.

Mesbur, E. S. (1991). Overview of baccalaureate field instruction: Objectives and outcomes. In D. Schneck, B. Grossman, & U. Glassman (Eds.), *Field instruction in social work: Contemporary issues and trends.* Dubuque, IA: Kendall/Hunt.

Reynolds, B. C. (1965). *Learning and teaching in the practice of social work.* New York: Russell & Russell.

Rosenblum, A. F., & Raphael, F. B. (1983). The role and function of the faculty field liaison. *Journal of Education for Social Work, 19*(1), 67–73.

Sikkema, M. (1966). A proposal for an innovation in field learning. In *Field instruction in graduate social work education: Old problems and new proposals.* New York: Council on Social Work Education.

Tolson, E. R., & Kopp, J. (1988). The practicum: Clients, problems, interventions, and influences on student practice. *Journal of Social Work Education, 24*(2), 123–134.

Additional Readings

Denton, W. H. (1992). What do field seminars accomplish? Student and instructor perspectives. *Journal of Teaching in Social Work, 6*(2), 59–73.

Skolnik, L. (1989). Field instruction in the 1980s: Realities, issues, and problem-solving strategies. In M. S. Raskin (Ed.), *Empirical studies in field instruction.* New York: Haworth Press.

White, H.R. (1988). Pros and cons of student placements with employers. *ARETE,* 13(2), 50–54.

Chapter **2**

The Partnership with Social Service Agencies

Overview

The intent of this chapter is to answer basic questions about social service agencies and field instructors who host and supervise social work students during their field instruction.

Why Do Agencies Accept Student Interns?

Social service agencies rarely receive direct financial incentives from colleges and universities to provide field experiences for their students. However, these agencies like being affiliated with teaching institutions—the training of students is stimulating and enriching for both the agency staff and the students involved. And there are secondary benefits. Most social service agencies are tremendously underfunded and have too many clients and too few staff. When there are not enough staff in an agency, students provide important and valued help. By using students to assist them, social work staff can focus on more problematic cases, or begin projects that have been put aside for lack of time. You should expect that the tasks assigned to you will be helpful to the agency. Additionally, the assignments given to students normally introduce students to the variety of tasks performed by social workers in the practicum setting.

Most social service agencies have a strong commitment to the training and development of future social workers. As well as helping to increase the number and quality of social work professionals, the agency finds that providing placements for students has two other advantages: First, the agency can screen, orient, train, and evaluate potential job applicants with a minimal investment in personnel costs. (It is not unusual for student interns to be offered employment by the agency when they have done a good job and when staff positions become vacant.)

Second, even if the agency cannot offer employment, it benefits by having a pool of future social workers in the community who are knowledgeable about the agency's services. Even though practicum students take jobs in other agencies, they will likely make referrals back to the practicum agency and, in general, will be better informed about the agency.

Beyond these reasons, staff within an agency may want to be field instructors because they enjoy teaching. They may find that their own practice skills are sharpened as they discuss with students various aspects of their practice. Furthermore, working with students can expose the agency staff to new developments in social work and help to relieve job fatigue.

How Are Field Agencies Chosen?

A human service agency may become a field instruction site for social work students in several ways. A faculty member, a social work practitioner in the community, or a student may recommend an agency. An agency may contact a social work program and request students. Or agencies may be approached directly by a faculty field liaison. Generally, agencies are expected to provide information on their programs, the learning experiences available to students, and the qualifications of the personnel available to supervise students. Faculty field liaisons look for agencies with such assets as: competent staff to provide effective supervision and professional learning; a commitment to social work ethics, values, and the training of social work professionals; diverse and broad programs compatible with the school's educational objectives; and adequate physical facilities (e.g., desk space, telephone access) to accommodate students.

Even agencies that have these qualifications may not become field agencies. Often, other factors such as the agency's reputation in the community, its leadership or innovation, and its climate (whether it is conducive to student learning) are considered. Some of the agencies that meet the above general criteria may become particularly attractive as field instruction sites because of considerations such as method of intervention, problem area of practice, population served, or availability of stipends for students.

After an agency has been found suitable for field instruction, the school and the agency frequently enter into a formal contractual agreement governing placement of students. Contained in the contract are the conditions, expectations, and terms of agreement that will be in effect during a student's practicum.

Some social work programs recommend that each field agency develop an outline for field instruction detailing important orientation items, assignments, and learning opportunities. Most social work programs maintain files on frequently used agencies for students' reference.

How Are Field Instructors Selected?

Although agency executive directors may recommend certain staff as supervisors for students, the faculty field liaison ultimately has the responsibility for determining who is qualified to supervise students. Criteria often include a master's degree from an accredited social work program and two to three years of postgraduate professional experience in a given practice area. It is also desirable that the field instructor have at least six months of experience within the particular agency. In some settings, the field instructor may be an experienced BSW. Beyond these primary requirements, the faculty field liaison looks for field instructors who have an interest in teaching and who are supportive of students. Field instructors must be knowledgeable, flexible individuals. They need to make time for overseeing students and for coordinating with faculty field liaisons. Field instructors tend to be among the most competent and energetic of an agency's staff. They incorporate the values and ethics of the profession and usually make excellent role models for students.

In order to know that field instructors meet the minimum requirements, social work programs usually ask for their résumés and maintain a file. However, just meeting the minimum requirements does not make a good field instructor. Field instructors who give students too little of their time, make unrealistic demands, or in other ways show themselves unable to assist students in their educational endeavors, may not be used again.

Case Example

Marcie's supervisor, Leesa, is the head of the social services department at a large hospital. Besides supervising 18 full-time and 12 part-time employees, the field instructor has a private practice. On three occasions Marcie's scheduled supervision time has been interrupted by emergency calls from Leesa's clients or other hospital business. However, Leesa has continued to give Marcie new admissions to follow. Marcie has been assigned 12 patients, but after one month has yet to receive any meaningful constructive feedback on her performance. Yesterday Leesa announced that she had been called to be an expert witness in a court case that could last several weeks. When Marcie asked if she could have another supervisor in Leesa's absence, Leesa laughed and said that Marcie should be "less compulsive."

Questions
1. Is Marcie's request unreasonable?
2. What options should Marcie explore?
3. Should this field instructor continue to be used?

How Are Agencies and Students Matched?

Frequently, students will have a preference for specific practicum settings. Some students know that they want to work with older adults when they graduate and desire to begin refining their skills with this population. Other students know that they want to work with children or in a medical setting. We believe that most faculty field liaisons try to place students in a practicum consistent with the students' first or second choice. However, what is paramount is that the experience be educational—that the student have opportunity for new learning and growth. In most programs, faculty field liaisons make the final decision.

Assuming that you have a preference (e.g., a mental health setting) and that your faculty field liaison will attempt to find you a practicum within this general area, what additional considerations are important? In our experience, faculty field liaisons give first consideration to the student's educational and learning needs. Faculty field liaisons must assess each student's specific needs and familiarity with the field of social work. Students who are knowledgeable or experienced in one area or type of agency should expect that they will be exposed to new activities (e.g., case management or advocacy) to help them to become well rounded. Students who want to dedicate all of their practicum experience to a specific population (e.g., psychiatric outpatients in a private practice clinic) may find that not every program will support their specialization. Philosophically, many faculty field liaisons believe that at least the first practicum ought to expose the student to a broad array of diverse clients. This is particularly true in undergraduate practicums.

Students who either have been employed in social service agencies or have extensive volunteer experience will generally be given placements where greater responsibility, knowledge, or judgment are required. Students who have had little or no exposure to social services will often be assigned to agencies where lack of previous experience will not be a disadvantage or a disservice to clients.

Less experienced students are not necessarily placed in situations where there will be limited exposure to client systems. These students can still expect significant contact, but in settings where there will be ample structure and supervision (e.g., assisting in a day treatment program for the chronically mentally ill). More experienced students will be able to function in situations where there is less structure or direct supervision. An example would be a respite program for senior citizens where (after a brief orientation period) students would be expected to travel to clients' homes to conduct assessments for the program.

In making assignments to agencies, faculty field liaisons also consider the individual student. A student who gives the appearance of being unorganized, or immature will most likely be placed in a less challenging practicum than a student considered organized, mature, and responsible. Of course, other traits or characteristics may also influence the faculty field liaison's decision. For instance, a confident and assertive student might be placed in a setting such as a locked psychiatric ward of a large hospital before a timid student would be.

Other factors that can affect the field placement include the student's unique learning style, characteristics, or disability, and can involve the faculty field liaison's contacts in the community. A faculty field liaison who is well known in the community may receive requests for students from local social service agencies. These requests can be rather specific. An agency with a shortage of male therapists might request a male student who enjoys working with adolescents. An after-school or day treatment program for children might request a student who is athletic and able to participate in strenuous sports such as swimming and backpacking. If you then come along with prior experience in scouting, recreational programming, or camping, the faculty field liaison could see you as a solution to meeting the agency's request. Faculty field liaisons know it is important to find students who meet social service agencies' needs so the training opportunities afforded by these agencies will continue to be available to future social work students. Such considerations may be responsible for students not getting their first, but a second or third, choice of a practicum.

What Specifically Are Social Service Agencies Looking for in Student Interns?

When interviewing students who are seeking practicum placements, agency supervisors tend to look for several characteristics: First is a strong desire on the part of the student to help others. Second is the student's interest and ability to deal with specific knowledge and skills relative to particular problem areas. Third is emotional maturity. Each of these will be briefly discussed.

A Strong Desire to Help Others. Most agency supervisors believe that the basic quality practicum students must have is a burning desire to help others. This desire should be a driving force in students' lives—they must feel it enough to keep trying even when it appears that a client wants to fail. Students must have a high tolerance for frustration. Social work can be discouraging, and students must be strongly motivated by the belief that clients want to help themselves. One agency supervisor explained,

> It is crucial to have the ability to be empathic with clients—to genuinely believe that clients are good people. Students must believe that clients love their children, that parents want to do what is best, and want to be appreciated. Without these beliefs, there is no way to make a social worker out of a student.

Agencies are looking for students who are determined, enthusiastic, and have genuine empathy for people. When a student displays attitudes that show condescension, you can be sure empathy is lacking. Students with empathy are easy to talk with, are good listeners, and are not cynical. They understand the client's world and the meaning it has for the client, both cognitively and emotionally.

> The client perceives the [student] acting in response to empathetic understanding when, in the client's words, "He was able to see and feel things in exactly the same way I do." "Many of the things she said just seemed to hit the nail on the head." "He understood my words but also how I felt." "When I did not know what I meant at all clearly, she still understood me." (Kadushin, 1990, p. 52)

Interest and Ability to Function in a Particular Setting. Agency interviewers seek students with genuine interest in the problem areas with which their organization deals. For example, an interest in addiction treatment is best displayed by a genuine desire to understand the human experience of addiction. Social service agencies do not want students who are fascinated by the complexity of clients' problems but who lack real interest in wanting to help them. Agencies want a student whose concern for a fellow human being is motivated by *both* an intellectual curiosity about the problem and a compassionate desire to help.

Particularly at the graduate level, agency supervisors may look for knowledge and skills in specific areas. For instance, a substance abuse treatment agency may expect students to already understand the disease model of alcoholism. Students seeking a macro or administrative placement may be expected by some agencies to have acquired knowledge of their clientele by having previously worked directly with these clients.

Maturity. Many agency supervisors try to assess the intellectual and emotional maturity displayed by a practicum applicant. Intellectually and emotionally mature individuals have achieved a balance between self-directed activity and a knowledge about the limitations of their competence. This is frequently displayed when applicants have formulated some clear objectives and are willing to seek advice and ask questions—even to say, "I don't understand."

Honesty. More and more agencies are fingerprinting new employees and running background checks with the police. If you have been arrested, this may or may not be a problem with your practicum agency depending on the type of offense and the length of time that has passed. Honesty is usually the best policy in these matters and maturity is demonstrated when you are able to reveal this type of information rather than leading agency personnel to believe you have never been in trouble with the law. If you have been arrested for a serious offense, you should discuss this with your faculty field liaison before going for interviews. You might also want to read the response to "Is it Wise to Admit My Weaknesses?" in Chapter 3.

Although agencies can have certain expectations about the qualities students need to possess before beginning an internship, the enthusiasm and interest you bring may have a strong influence. Also, it is often important to get ready for your interview by jotting down a few ideas about why you want to work with a particular group of clients, how you have prepared yourself for the practicum, and examples demonstrating past responsibilities you have handled. See also the topic in Chapter 3 "How Do I Prepare for the Practicum Interview?"

Case Example

You have a friend, Heather, in the social work program. Heather always seems to be too busy for her own good. Typically, she runs a day or two late in turning in major assignments. She is working full time and also going to school full time. She seems to be getting only four or five hours of sleep each night. Still, she is active in several volunteer organizations around town. Heather tells the faculty field liaison that she is working only part time on weekends.

Possibly because she failed to note it on her calendar, Heather missed a day she was scheduled to work at her practicum agency. The next time she appeared, her field instructor inquired whether she had been too ill to call in. Heather was momentarily flustered as she tried to recall what she had been doing. Not wanting the field instructor to know that she was really working a full-time job, Heather made up a flimsy excuse.

Heather also had a problem turning in required agency paperwork within the deadlines her field instructor gave. Now, at the midterm evaluation, the field instructor is suggesting to the faculty field liaison that Heather be terminated.

Heather is confused, hurt, and angry. She has been trying her best, she thinks, although she dislikes the clients she has to work with.

Questions

1. What do you consider to be Heather's biggest problem?
2. What could Heather have done to improve her situation in the agency?

How Will the Agency Evaluate My Performance as a Student Intern?

Although the evaluation procedures used by different agencies and social work programs vary widely, you can expect that your field instructor will be looking at your progress during the placement. Field instructors often use prepared forms or scales to rate students on their knowledge, skills, and social work values. These forms may be supplied by your faculty field liaison or may have been developed at the agency. Field instructors generally discuss their written evaluations with students or give students the opportunity to review their comments and respond. In some programs, faculty field liaisons attend the evaluation session. During your orientation to the agency or to the field practicum, you may be given a copy of the evaluation form that will be used. If a copy is not supplied, ask for one so that you can be familiar with the areas in which you will be expected to show improvement. (More discussion of this topic is provided in Chapter 4.)

In addition to the skills and knowledge you are expected to acquire, certain other qualities are necessary: Foremost are good attendance and being on time for your appointments and scheduled days. You may be considered unreliable if your attendance is poor (even if you have good excuses). Other qualities that agencies like in student interns include a pleasant disposition, willingness to work (sometimes expressed as interest in helping others when not busy with your own assignments), a sense of humor, sensible (businesslike) appearance, and sincerity in learning. Furthermore, agencies want students who are in control of their emotions, who are calm and objective (even under stressful conditions), who have good judgment, and who are appropriately assertive.

Most field instructors will rate more highly those student interns who have qualities that would make them good employees once the practicum is finished. As suggested earlier, these would be individuals who get along easily with their coworkers and clients, who are hard working, conscientious, and responsible. Student interns who are willing to help out no matter what the task, and those considered to be an asset to the agency (perhaps because they have developed a special expertise or have found a niche for themselves in the agency), are favored by field instructors and agency administrators.

Here are some other guidelines to help you get along with your field instructor and other staff within the agency:

- Do not try to impress agency workers with vocabulary that you have just learned.
- When you communicate in writing, use good grammar and spelling and try to write legibly. (If you can't spell well, don't guess—use a dictionary or spellchecker faithfully.)

- Listen carefully to any instructions given to you the first time and make notes if necessary. Do not make a practice of going back to the agency supervisor on multiple occasions to ask for information that has already been given to you. However, if you need further instructions or information to complete your assignments, then it is more responsible to ask for help than to finish an assignment incorrectly.
- Do not give your field instructor the impression that you are picky about the assignments you will take. If you are not being given enough work, don't be afraid to ask for additional duties.
- Once you have been given responsibility for something, then carry it out. Do not draw out tasks; do not forget assignments.
- Be on time and keep appointments.
- If you borrow something, then return it. Show consideration to others. Do not leave a mess for others to clean.
- If there are personality clashes or personnel problems within the agency, try not to get involved. Avoid agency gossip or discussion that you perceive to be about the faults or flaws of selected agency employees.
- If you develop a significant problem with a coworker within the agency, then share this information with your faculty field liaison as soon as possible. Conform to the National Association of Social Workers' Code of Ethics (1996)—do not engage in unethical behavior.
- Keep a positive attitude. Even if the agency does not conform to your ideal image, considerable learning can occur in every practicum. If you have decided (or even if you and your faculty field liaison have decided) that a different placement is necessary next semester, do not adopt the attitude that you will do just enough to get by. (One worthwhile reason to try your best is that you might want your field instructor to write a good letter of reference for a future job.)

If you truly want to learn and to help the clientele of your agency, then you will almost certainly meet most of the agency's performance standards and receive a positive evaluation.

Printed with the permission of Chris Rosenthal.

What Do I Do if the Field Instructor Becomes Incapacitated?

Occasionally, events such as accidents, illnesses, or planned absences may mean that your field instructor is unable to continue with your supervision. Your field instructor and faculty field liaison should have enough time to make alternative arrangements for planned absences (e.g., vacations). However, your faculty field liaison may not always know when your field instructor is unavailable to supervise you because of unplanned absences such as an accident or illness. In this situation, it is your responsibility to inform your faculty field liaison of such absences—particularly when it is likely that more than one supervisory session will be missed.

Ideas for Enriching the Practicum Experience

1. What characteristics or features of a social service agency do you think are essential for it to be a practicum setting for social work students? Jot down your ideas and compare them with the ideas of your fellow students enrolled in the integrating seminar. Alternatively, save your list and examine it at the end of the placement to see if any of your ideas have changed.

2. If you were the supervisor of students in a social service agency, what kinds of attitudes, abilities, and knowledge would you expect them to acquire during their field instruction? How close do these come to the criteria that will be used to evaluate you? Obtain a copy of the evaluation form that your field instructor or faculty field liaison will use and compare.

3. Determine if your social work program keeps students' evaluations of their practicum agencies. If so, read student remarks about the agencies that interest you. Which sound like serious concerns? If your program does not systematically collect evaluations on the practicum settings, determine if there is enough interest to begin gathering this information at the end of each academic term.

4. What agencies are used most often for practicum settings by your social work program? Are different agencies used for undergraduate and graduate field experiences? Is there a good balance in terms of fields of service (e.g., child welfare, mental health, gerontology)?

5. If the résumés for the field instructors used by your social work program are available, examine several to understand the diversity and richness of their experiences and special expertise. Do you see yourself having a similar résumé in another eight to ten years? Make a list of your career goals.

References

Kadushin, A. (1972). *The social work interview*. New York: Columbia University Press.
National Association of Social Workers. *Code of Ethics*, 1996. Washington,D.C.: National Association of Social Workers.

Additional Readings

Bogo, M. & Globerman, J. (1995). Creating effective university-field partnerships: An analysis of two inter-organization models for field education. *Journal of Teaching in Social Work, 11,* 177–192.

Gelman, S. R. (1990). The crafting of fieldwork training agreements. *Journal of Social Work Education, 26*(1), 65–75.

Hancock, T. U. (1992). Field placements in for-profit agencies: Policies and practices of graduate programs. *Journal of Social Work Education, 28*(3), 330–340.

Hepworth, D. H., & Larsen, J. A. (1990). Negotiating goals and formulating a contract. In *Direct social work practice: Theory and skills* (pp. 336–371). Belmont, CA: Wadsworth.

Rosenfeld, D. J. (1989). Field instructor turnover. In Miriam S. Raskin (Ed.), *Empirical studies in field instruction.* New York: Haworth Press.

Chapter **3**

Getting Started

Overview

Most students want their practicum experiences to be instructive, exciting, and gratifying. But before the practicum can start, the student often must be interviewed in the agency. Even if an interview is not required, the student is likely to be a little nervous about getting off on the right foot and making a good impression. This chapter provides some suggestions for students preparing to go into an agency for the first time.

How Do I Find an Agency that Meets My Needs?

The amount of student input allowed in the choice of a practicum agency varies immensely. On the one extreme in some social work programs, students are not just permitted to contact agencies and interview on their own, but expected to do so. Students in these programs often talk to other students and faculty members about which agencies provide the best learning experiences. If, for some reason, you are unable to secure a placement in one of the agencies most often recommended (possibly because they already have their quota of students), you may want to look through the Yellow Pages of your phone directory (or even the directories of neighboring counties if travel time isn't an issue). Under such headings as "Counselors," "Social Service Organizations," "Marriage Counseling," "Mental Health Services," or "Alcohol Abuse & Addiction" you are likely to find more agencies than you had imagined. In addition, your local United Way will have a list of agencies it funds, and it may produce a directory of community resources. Such a publication would likely contain more information about individual agencies than you would find in the Yellow Pages. Check in the reference section of your library.

In programs at the other extreme, students are assigned an agency and have little choice. Most programs allow students to state preferences even if they are not actively involved in the selection process. Correspondingly, most agencies want to interview prospective students before agreeing to accept them for a placement.

Even if your program does not allow you to choose your practicum agency, there are several important topics to consider as you plan for a practicum. Occasionally students or agencies have special requirements, and discussing them with your faculty field liaison will result in a better learning experience. Here are a few examples:

Transportation. Getting to and from the agency can be a problem for students without a car. Students need to consider how close the agency is located to where they live and go to class. Many agencies are located near college campuses and are easy to reach. Others are some distance away and require ownership of a car, availability of public transportation, or arrangements for car pooling with other students or employees.

If you have a car or access to one, some agencies may ask you to use your car to transport clients or make home visits. Other agencies have cars available for student use. If you are required to drive an agency car, you might want to ask your agency supervisor about the extent of insurance coverage needed to protect you in case of an accident. If you drive your own car, you need to check with your insurance agent about your liability coverage.

Scheduling. Agencies differ with regard to hours of operation, from those open only a few days per week (this is often the case with new agencies or those that operate almost entirely with volunteers) to those that provide intervention 24 hours per day, seven days per week.

Some students can be very flexible as they plan their agency time. Others must work around job responsibilities and family commitments and are far less adaptable. Agencies are aware of these differences, and although some are able to accommodate students' schedules, others simply cannot. Students whose schedules are restricted must find agencies that are open at times they can work.

Even if your schedule appears to have no complications (e.g., your classes are on Tuesdays and Thursdays and the agency agrees to accept you as a student on Mondays, Wednesdays, and Fridays), be alert to potential problems such as staff meetings on Tuesday afternoons—a day when you are not scheduled to be in the agency. This circumstance would probably necessitate that you consider a different agency because staff meetings are an important experience in professional socialization. In staff meetings students can observe how the agency operates, how professionals interact with one another, and learn what problems are facing the agency and how they will be resolved.

Supervision. Some students want agency expectations laid out in clear and behaviorally specific terms. They want to know what to do, when to do it, and how to do it. They do not like wondering whether or not they are meeting agency expectations. One student explained,

> Prior to my first day at work, I was surprised to find that I was feeling anxious. My anxiety was based on a fear that there might be little or no structure, that I might have to roam aimlessly, searching for assignments and feeling generally uncomfortable with my new situation.

Other students want a setting in which they can observe for a while, determine what they would like to do, and then begin to use all of their creative and problem-solving capabilities in a task of their choosing.

When selecting an agency, it is important to consider the amount of supervision you require. The next step is to share this preference with your faculty field liaison. From prior experience with other students, your faculty field liaison will know which agencies allow employees, students, and volunteers the most freedom and which provide greater supervision.

One undergraduate student, who was placed in an unstructured environment with little supervision, arrived at a day-care center for high-risk children and was told that 15 toddlers were in the next room. She was instructed to go and assist in any way she could. A second undergraduate working in an agency that distributed food to 16 out-lying food pantries was given a detailed questionnaire and asked to interview one social worker at each site to gather information on anticipated food requirements. Still a third undergraduate, in a very structured setting, walked into her agency supervisor's office and was given a schedule of training sessions to be held that week for all hospital student interns. She was assigned specific areas of the hospital in which to work, specific tasks to complete, deadlines by which to accomplish the assignments, and a schedule of supervisory conferences. She was told to begin reading hospital policies and logs of former students. Later, she viewed a video on the hospital's history and projected future.

These examples show how problems might develop for students who want a lot of supervision and who do not get it, or who like to work on their own but whose agency supervisors closely observe and direct their activities. It is important to communicate your preference concerning the degree of supervision, or problems may quickly arise and continue throughout the placement. What you want in a supervisor is a supportive, enthusiastic, knowledgeable person who is interested in helping you to have a good learning experience. A good supervisor will not abandon or ignore you, will find interesting assignments for you, and will be available for your questions.

Agencies vary widely with regard to what they will allow students to do. Some schedule immediate contact with clients; others do not allow students to have client interaction without supervision until the second semester. One graduate student told a class of undergraduates going into the field for the first time, "Be prepared for the possibility of spending the initial weeks in your agencies doing nothing but observing." She noted that as a second-year graduate student, with six years of social work experience and one graduate practicum completed, she was told by her new field instructor that for the first month her only assignment was to observe others at work. The second month she could interview clients but only with another social worker present. Finally, at the start of her third month, assuming things went to the supervisor's satisfaction, she could practice alone.

Most agencies are not this stringent in their supervision of students and present students with opportunities to interact with clients early in their internships—sometimes even in the first week. This occurs at both the graduate and undergraduate levels. The variation in students' direct contact with clients can be explained by many factors, among them the staff-client ratio, the complexity of the students' tasks, and the consequences of students making poor judgments.

Populations, Problem Areas, and Networking. Ideally, students should find placements where they can learn about populations and problem areas that excite them. The agency you select should capture your interests and challenge you to become actively involved. Although it is possible to learn something in any placement, students are most energized when they can immediately immerse themselves in a setting where they easily relate to the primary client group present (e.g., preschoolers, adolescents, elderly) or are curious about the problems with which the agency deals (e.g., chemical dependency, teenage runaways, spouse abuse, juvenile offenders, the terminally ill). Especially before the first placement, students should reflect on what their areas of interest are and which age groups they interact with best.

Agencies that do more networking are more interrelated with other agencies, and thus provide a broader practicum experience. Students who want to learn about other social service organizations and the interactions among them should consider how much networking a particular agency does. For example, a family counseling agency that works almost entirely with middle income families may have little cause to work with other agencies in the community. On the other hand, an agency that works with pregnant teens will make connections with social insurance agencies, county or state social service departments, health departments, hospital social service departments, childbirth education organizations, legal services, and residential facilities. Students interested in maximizing their knowledge about other agencies and community resources would receive more of this type of learning in the latter example.

Agency Value Base. Another area for students to consider is an agency's value base. Once students identify the core values of a potential field agency, they should decide whether it creates a conflict with their own. For example, a student who believes that abortion is morally wrong will have a difficult time working in a setting where clients are often referred for abortions. Likewise, a student whose religious ethic is opposed to divorce may have difficulties in a setting where persons are frequently supported in leaving their spouses.

Often our clients' values may not be the same as ours. As professionals, we learn to accept individual clients as worthwhile persons although we may not condone their every behavior. Although it is important to know our strongly held values and to examine them from time to time, it is also worth remembering that values are not permanently fixed. Many people, particularly those acquiring college degrees, are continually updating the facts that form the foundation for their opinions and values. A 19-year-old undergraduate may strongly believe in the death penalty, thinking that certain incarcerated individuals deserve this punishment. With this value, that student may not be very successful in some criminal justice placements. However, a short time later, the same student may have learned that the poor and minorities have a much greater likelihood of ending up on death row. Seeing the evidence of racism within the legal system, the student may now view the death penalty quite differently.

In the process of obtaining a social work education, students become aware of their own basic values and the values of the profession, and they are challenged to understand the impact of their values on their interactions with others. Personal and professional growth occur when we examine our values and the stereotypes we hold. However, students should not be forced to act against their basic principles. In such a situation or at any time when you cannot be objective, you should inform your field instructor and discuss transferring or referring the case. If this poses any problem, a three-way meeting with your faculty field liaison, field instructor, and you should be convened.

How Do I Prepare for the Practicum Interview?

Anticipation of the initial interview with a prospective agency supervisor can produce anxiety. One undergraduate student recalled,

> I phoned the executive director of the agency and arranged for an interview. In the day or two before I was to see her, I unexpectedly discovered that I was feeling quite nervous. Upon examining my feelings, I found that I feared such things as: They won't like me. I won't like them. They will find my dress too casual. I will find them too snooty. All of these fears could be categorized under a basic "fear of the unknown."
>
> To my surprise, the interview went very well. The director talked about the agency and its purpose and her ideas about students' roles. She asked me about my background and interest in social work and she shared some personal experiences about her own agency work. Before I knew it, an hour had passed. It was a relief to know rapport had definitely been established between us.

Not all first interviews go nearly as well. One student recalled how she was caught totally off guard:

> When I was interviewing for a practicum placement last semester, I was asked what would seem to be a simple question. However, the manner in which the question was asked intimidated me. The interviewer, a stern looking middle-aged clinical social worker, folded her hands, looked me straight in the eye, and asked, "Yesterday I interviewed another student. Tell me why I should choose you over other students?" I remember frantically trying to think of a good reason. I'm sure my voice was shaking when I asked her to repeat the question (I wanted to stall for time). I ended up giving her two or three reasons, none of which sounded very convincing to me. From then on I was unnerved. When I left the interview, that question was about the only thing I could remember!

Although there is no way to guarantee that your first interview with a potential agency supervisor will be a fun experience, a few steps can be taken to increase the likelihood of a positive experience. Many people find it hard to speak extemporaneously about their strengths, weaknesses, qualifications, career goals, skills, and abilities. For example, some students may find it difficult to answer the following questions:

- What led you to social work?
- Why do you think you are qualified to be a student intern at this agency?
- How would you describe yourself?
- What talents do you have?
- What do you plan on doing five or ten years from now?
- What skills can you bring to our agency?

- Why should we consider you as a student intern?
- What problems do you think will be most difficult for you to deal with in this agency setting?

Yet these questions and others may be asked during your interview. Fortunately, you can prepare for questions such as these.

Making a detailed self-assessment is one way to prepare for an interview. You should be able to describe traits and skills that contribute to your uniqueness. You might begin by compiling a list of flattering adjectives that characterize you (e.g., ambitious, trustworthy, reliable, compassionate, intellectual). Next, narrow the list to three or four items that summarize your personality. Use examples to illustrate particular attributes (e.g., one undergraduate described himself as "committed" and then explained how he continued working for a summer youth camp during a three-week period when funding shortages meant he did not receive any pay). Once you have specific attributes and examples in mind, it is fairly easy to respond to the request, "describe yourself."

Trace skills (e.g., the ability to work in stressful situations) to concrete, specific experiences. Describe a particular experience to show how you have used this skill (e.g., you managed an office for two weeks by yourself while other office personnel were on leave). You should be deliberate in describing a strength relative to the position sought (e.g., knowledge of medical terminology when seeking a practicum within a hospital setting). As attorneys do in a courtroom, you want to "build a case"—present "evidence" that you actually possess the traits and skills you say you have.

What Can I Do to Deemphasize Little or No Work Experience?

Both graduate and undergraduate students worry that they will be asked about their lack of practical experience. This anxiety sometimes blocks the memory of experiences that are related to the demands of the desired practicum. To avoid overlooking relevant experiences, consider your significant past activities before the interview. Perhaps you did volunteer work, were employed in a family business, or were a member of a community service or school organization. Next, make a list of the skills you needed to complete assignments in those settings. You are now ready to link your past with what the current agency needs.

Begin by telling the interviewer what you have done in the past. Next, use a transitional statement to link the past to the present. An undergraduate student gave the following example:

> As leader of my daughter's Girl Scout troop for two years, I coordinated group activities for eight- and nine-year-olds. I found I was organized and creative. I think I would be able to build upon this experience when working here in the after-school program.

Even jobs that were not social work related (e.g., working in a supermarket) show that you have learned how to balance schoolwork and other responsibilities, and more likely than not, you picked up valuable skills in working with people.

Case Example

A student in one of your classes begins to share some personal material with you. She was a victim of severe child abuse and reared by foster parents. Although she has never received any individual counseling, she now wants to do a practicum that will place her on a treatment team for children who have been sexually abused. Previously, other students who have completed a practicum with this agency have told you how intense and stressful their placement was. The student who wants to go to this agency hints that such a field experience will be "therapeutic" for her.

Questions

1. Do you think her plan for a practicum is a good one?
2. Would you advise her to choose a different practicum?
3. On what might your decision depend?
4. Would it be a good idea for the student to inform her field instructor and faculty field liaison of her prior history?

Is it Wise to Admit My Weaknesses?

In an interview, agency supervisors may ask potential student interns to describe their weaknesses. Questions such as these are asked: What weaknesses do you have? What aspect of this placement do you think will be the most difficult? What is the biggest hindrance you will have to deal with if we select you as a student intern? To prepare for this type of question, consider any potential weaknesses you may have and then rehearse a response using one of the following approaches.

One method is to accentuate the positive. One student remembered,

> When asked what my weaknesses were relative to the placement, I knew that I did not want to focus on any anticipated problems; so I said that I thought my organization, willingness, and flexibility would enable me to handle any difficult situations I might encounter.

A second approach is to state a weakness and then reframe it into a trait that is positive. One student did this in an interview by saying, "Some people would say that I push myself too hard but I like to think of myself as someone who strives for excellence." As another example of reframing, a student said, "People may think I do not grasp things quickly enough, but I spend a lot of time trying to completely understand. I find this often helps me to save time in the long run."

A third way to deal with the subject of weaknesses is to explain how you are working on a particular liability and illustrate specific instances in which you have been encouraged by progress. During a practicum interview, a student explained that she gets very nervous speaking in front of a group. She is working on this by taking a public speaking course.

Occasionally, students have questions about whether or not medical diagnoses should be mentioned during an interview at an agency. A student with epilepsy informed his faculty field liaison of this, and together they were able to find a placement where staff were well-prepared if the student had a seizure. Had the agency supervisor not known that the student's medical condition was the reason for his reluctance to do certain work (e.g., transporting clients), the supervisor might have thought the student was uncooperative.

If you are presently in counseling for an emotional problem, or have been in the recent past, it may be wise to share this information with the faculty field liaison so that the two of you can decide on the best placement for you. It generally is not advised, for instance, for victims of incest or sexual abuse to begin counseling others with the same problem until considerable progress has been made in their own treatment. Similarly, students from alcoholic families should be pretty far into their own recovery before seeking to work intensively with alcoholic clients. Sharing this type of information with the faculty field liaison does not indicate any weakness on your part; it shows maturity and good judgment in dealing with a sometimes painful reality.

How much personal information about students should be shared with agencies is a thorny dilemma for faculty field liaisons. For example, if a student has a criminal record, fails to inform the agency of this, and then violates the law again (either harming clients, putting clients at risk, or causing the agency bad publicity), the issue of liability is raised. On the other hand, disclosing this type of information to agencies will undoubtedly induce some to reject a student. Sharing too much information with an agency may not be in the student's best interest.

In general, students should advise their faculty field liaisons of medical conditions or other situations that could affect their agency work or have repercussions for the agency. The faculty field liaison and the student can then jointly decide whether and to what degree to inform the agency. There are no simple rules on this matter; the advantages and disadvantages of revealing personally sensitive information must be weighed in each individual situation. It is always a delicate issue, but it can be handled successfully with adequate planning.

Consider the following example of how to inform an agency about these matters:

A student who was on medication for a bipolar disorder discussed this with her faculty field liaison, and the two of them decided on an agency where she would learn needed skills and also receive supervision from an understanding and perceptive agency supervisor. No exceptional information was given to the agency supervisor ahead of time. The student went through the interview the same as any student would, and she and the agency supervisor developed good rapport during the interview. As the interview was drawing to a close, the agency supervisor announced that he was favorably impressed and informed the student that she could begin a placement with the agency. At that time, the student revealed her medication needs but added that she felt secure this would not present a problem to the agency. The supervisor asked a couple of questions for clarification. The student did not go into a detailed history, but answered factually regarding her behavior when she was acting symptomatically and reassured the supervisor that over the past 18 months she had been functioning well—missing fewer days of school than others. The supervisor thanked the student for her honesty and began discussing when the student would be available to start the practicum.

In this example, information was not given ahead of time in order not to bias the supervisor against the student. Since the interview had gone well, the student felt comfortable in disclosing. Had the student felt that the interview was not going well and that it was unlikely that she would be invited to join the agency for a practicum, then the faculty field liaison and the student agreed that disclosure was not necessary.

How Should I Respond to Questions About My Educational Preparation?

In a practicum interview, you may be asked to explain how your classroom learning will apply to the particular agency setting. Although you cannot foresee every specific question that might be asked, you can prepare by anticipating related questions and mentally reviewing your educational preparation. The following example shows how a little preparation can give you poise and confidence:

> A graduate student tried to locate a placement that would improve his counseling skills. He contacted an acquaintance at a local community mental health center and inquired about the possibility of an internship. The acquaintance, the director of the agency, seemed interested and supportive but suggested that the student attend the next "team" meeting at the center and make the request at that time. Not wishing to seem impolite, the student wondered why he would have to make the request a second time but did not seek further explanation. Since he and the director already knew each other from membership in a local organization, the student assumed that the way was smoothed for him to become an intern—only the details would need to be worked out.
>
> On the appointed day, the naive student arrived bright and early but was made to wait outside of the meeting room until "agency business" was concluded. When the meeting ran late, the student began to suspect that team members were arguing about the merits of accepting him as an intern. Finally, after waiting 40 minutes, the student was invited to enter the meeting.
>
> The director made the initial introductions and indicated that the student wanted to become an intern. Then he said, "Tell us something about yourself and your program." The student patiently spoke of his career goals, hobbies, and so on. Somehow this did not seem to be what the team wanted. The student had thought that by now he would be at the end of the interview. However, one of the team members then said, "No, what we want to know is what theoretical approaches do you use when you counsel?" The student's mind raced. Systems theory, reality therapy, Gestalt, and psychoanalysis came to mind. He wondered if he really knew enough about any of them. After several false starts, the student said, "I think I'm eclectic."

The point of this illustration is that students should give prior thought to the types of things (e.g., their training or counseling frame of reference) that may interest the interviewer or interviewing staff in the prospective agency.

Interviewers ask questions about educational backgrounds for many reasons. They may be trying to assess intellectual abilities, breadth and depth of knowledge, or special interests or training. To get ready for any questioning along this line, think about your educational experience and then write down two or three courses that were valuable preparation for this specific practicum placement. Next, think of theories or concepts discussed in these courses and write down why you think each would be helpful. This exercise will enable you to go into the interview mindful of important concepts and theories. Interviewers will not expect you to recite an entire course syllabus. However, being able to recall two or three major theories and explain how they relate to the work of the agency would impress many interviewers.

What if the general questions are, "What kind of program do they run there at your university? Is it a good one?" To answer these questions, think about two or three aspects of your social work program that have given you good preparation. For example, some programs incorporate a social work course that requires students to perform a few hours of agency volunteer work each week. This educational experience helps a student know what to expect and what to do in a practicum and could be described as a program strength.

Be positive in describing the valuable learning acquired from your educational experience. An educational program that is described chiefly in negative terms may be seen by some interviewers as inadequately preparing you to function in their agency—as a student or as an employee.

How Should I Dress for the Practicum Agency?

As with many things in life, it is best to avoid extremes. Whether going for the first interview or reporting for work on the first day, you should not plan to make a fashion statement. Provocative dress will not be acceptable and may result in losing a placement that you desired. Generally speaking, dress conservatively, but neither too formally nor informally. If possible, visit the agency beforehand and observe what other staff members are wearing. If the staff dresses informally (men in sports shirts without ties; women in slacks and casual tops), then dress similarly. If your supervisor and other staff are dressed a little fancier, then use them as models and dress appropriately. Do not wear jeans on the first interview. Later, if you become an intern there and learn that jeans are typical dress because of the agency population or setting (e.g., assisting clients in a sheltered workshop), then it is usually permissible to wear jeans. When in doubt, dress up a little more than you normally would for going to class.

Keep in mind, too, that clothes which would be considered attractive and stylish in a normal business office might be viewed as being provocative if, for example, you are working in a prison with male inmates. Plan your dress to avoid getting "noticed" and always ask ahead of time if you have questions about appropriate apparel.

How Do I Make a Good Impression?

Most initial interviews will last only 30 to 60 minutes. Use this time to make a positive impression by remembering a few simple but important details. First, plan to arrive 10 to 15 minutes early. It is always better to be early for an important appointment than to be late. If you plan to arrive early, then even unexpected delays can be absorbed without major problems.

Second, when you meet the prospective agency supervisor, look the person in the eyes and offer a firm handshake. Smile and show a genuine interest in the person. Take care to pronounce the supervisor's name correctly (if you are unsure, ask). Be prepared to spend the first few minutes making small talk. If you have not been keeping up with current events, read the local newspaper and a national magazine prior to your meeting. This can help to give you topics for discussion should the conversation move past your credentials. This could easily happen, for example, if your interview was scheduled for 11:15 and the agency supervisor invites you to lunch.

Third, be observant. Look around the office or room and note anything of particular interest to you. One student noticed a guitar sitting in a corner and quickly engaged the supervisor in a discussion about their shared interest in classical guitar. Meeting strangers is always a little difficult at first. By facilitating conversation with the interviewer, you can demonstrate a skill that will later be required with clients. You will leave a better impression if both you and the interviewer can speak comfortably than if you appear frightened and hesitant to talk.

Fourth, show enthusiasm. One way to do this is to ask questions. Do not be completely passive and think your role is only to wait for questions. Ask questions about the agency, the staff, the clientele, how long the supervisor has been with the agency, and so on. You can ask what formal training is given to students, how student performance is appraised, and what student responsibilities are. Furthermore, you can inquire about what staff you will be working with, the primary functions of the office, and the expected working hours.

Students can usually generate interesting discussion if they have acquired some basic information about the agency before the interview, such as:

- The relative size of the agency (Has it added or lost staff recently?)
- Its organizational auspices (Is it a private or public agency? Where do most of its funds come from?)
- The array of services provided to clients (Who is the "typical" client?)
- Recent news pertaining to the organization (Have there been any recent newspaper articles?)

During the interview, show congruence between your verbal and nonverbal communication. Modulate your voice to maintain the interviewer's attention and be sure to keep appropriate posture. Try to avoid saying what you will not do (e.g., "I will *never* work past 4:30"); rather, emphasize your congeniality and flexibility.

Finally, keep in mind that many agency supervisors are asking questions in the hopes of answering the following:

- What can you do for the agency?
- How long will it take you to become productive?
- What do you want from the agency?
- Can you handle stress?
- Can you get along with others?

By anticipating questions that interviewers are likely to ask and by knowing the "hidden agenda," there is a better chance that you will leave a good impression than if you go unprepared.

A day or two after your interview, it would be a nice touch to drop the potential field instructor a brief thank-you note in the mail expressing appreciation for interviewing you. If you schedule three or four interviews, and each agency offers you the opportunity to come there and be an intern, it is always expected that as soon as you have made a decision you will call and inform the other agencies. They may be waiting to hear from you before committing to any other students. Once again, thank them for their interest and assistance.

Getting Oriented—What Can I Expect on the First Day?

Agencies prepare for and use students in enormously different ways. Two accounts illustrate this:

> The first day in one of my graduate practicums another student and I were handed a scrapbook of clippings about the agency and instructed to familiarize ourselves with the agency's range of activities. We carefully pored over the scrapbook and about 15 minutes later returned it to our supervisor and asked what we should do next. With a look of surprise he informed us that he thought the activity would have taken us most of the day. He actually had made no other plans for us on the first day, and said that we could go home. Looking back on this experience now, I realize that very little planning had gone on prior to our arrival.

Another student experienced something quite different:

> I participated in a training session aimed at familiarizing new students with various facets of the agency. The director, codirector, two experienced volunteers, and one agency worker conducted the seminar. Several topics related to agency operations were discussed, such as the importance of confidentiality, agency policies, forms, and procedures.

The atmosphere created by the staff in the latter example enabled the student to feel comfortable about making comments and asking questions. A large part of the training was devoted to role playing by the staff. They acted out several typical cases, demonstrating a variety of likely occurrences. In summary the student commented,

> At the end of the session, we were given the opportunity to assess the worth of the training. I offered my positive comments and left the meeting feeling I had been treated with respect, appreciation, and a genuine concern. The staff seemed to provide me with the knowledge necessary for a productive learning experience.

These examples illustrate differences in orientation. Ideally, the first day and perhaps the first week should be closer to the second example. Your orientation should include an introduction to the agency (e.g., its mission and services), the staff, and the physical layout of the facility, and an explanation of pertinent agency policies and procedures. However, agency staff members may be pulled away to take care of client emergencies or to attend to other crises within an agency. Occasionally, agency supervisors simply have not planned or do not have the time to provide activities that will be meaningful or fully involve students on their first day. One student expressed her frustration this way:

My first day in the practicum my supervisor had gone to a workshop and had forgotten that I was coming. I lost three days that I had planned on working there because he was unavailable. His secretary offered to give me some filing to do, but I decided to come back the following week. I've done secretarial work, I wanted to learn how to be a social worker.

The best supervisors thoughtfully anticipate and plan experiences for students to gain new perspectives and insights into the social work profession while helping with the work that needs to be done. And although it is not uncommon for "disasters" to occur during a student's initial orientation to an agency, settings where there is too little planning, insufficient supervision, and too much chaos do not provide students with the necessary structure. If these terms characterize your placement, you should address this problem by speaking with your faculty field liaison.

How Do I Develop a Learning Contract?

You will probably be given the opportunity to develop contracts with clients in your practicum. To become familiar with the use of contracts, most social work programs will expect you to prepare a learning (or educational) contract of your own—one that outlines your responsibilities in the practicum. This three-way agreement usually involves you, the field instructor, and the faculty field liaison and generally states what you hope to learn from the practicum (i.e., your goals), the responsibilities or tasks that will be given to you, and miscellaneous details such as the amount or extent of supervision you will receive and the hours or days that you will be in the practicum agency. Usually, the three parties will sign and receive a copy of the contract.

The learning contract minimizes the possibility of misunderstandings and provides a basis for accountability. It helps students keep in mind what they have committed themselves to, provides a sense of progress and satisfaction as portions of it are completed, and helps students to plan their time in the agency. The learning contract supplies necessary safeguards to ensure the integrity of the practicum as an educational experience and to discourage the use of students as substitute employees.

Start working on the learning contract by familiarizing yourself with the practicum requirements of your program and the agency's expectations of you. (Sometimes, all the students in a given agency are expected to meet certain learning goals, and these may already be stated for you.) Read the practicum syllabus or manual. For example, how many days or hours are you expected to be in the agency each week? Compare your learning needs and career goals with the educational opportunities that will be afforded to you in this placement. Then, draft a set of goals and objectives that you hope to achieve in this practicum.

Note that a distinction has been made between goals and objectives. *Goals* provide a general sense of direction—the target for which you are aiming. For instance, you might have the goal of learning how to make differential psychiatric diagnoses. Or, you might write a goal to develop skills to work with adolescents in groups.

Objectives follow from your goals and may be thought of as stepping stones—that is, activities that help you reach your goals. Objectives should always be expressed so that it is easy to monitor whether or not they were accomplished. Therefore, objectives need to be both measurable and attainable. It is helpful to use action verbs, to specify a time or date within the objective when a task should be accomplished, and when possible, to identify quantities.

After you have listed your goals for the practicum, think of each active step, activity, or responsibility that you will have to undertake or perform. These will suggest to you the objectives that should fall under each learning goal. Of these tasks or activities, choose the ones that are most directly observable and whose feedback will be essential to your field education. For each objective ask, "How will my field instructor know that I have achieved this objective?"

Usually it is enough to identify three or four goals that you would like to work toward and two or three related objectives. Each objective achieved should help your field instructor know that you have made progress toward reaching a goal. If it will be difficult or impossible to know when you have completed an objective, then the objective is not useful; it needs to be rewritten in more behavioral terms. Finally, consider how much time it will take to achieve the objective. If it will take more time than is available to you, then you must discard it. You should have a mixture of a few objectives that can be met within the first several weeks of the practicum, and others that will not be completed until the last several weeks.

When you are satisfied with the rough draft of your learning contract, share it with your field instructor, and the two of you can then make any necessary revisions. After incorporating the revisions and retyping the document, you may be ready for signatures. However, ask whether or not your faculty field liaison wants to review the contract before obtaining the signature of the field instructor. It is probably best if you do not think of the contract as being in its final form until it has been reviewed by both the field instructor and the faculty field liaison. When there are no further revisions, you and the field agency and school representatives will sign the learning contract. Each of these parties should then receive a copy of the agreement.

There is no single best approach to contract development. However, the SPIRO model (Pfeiffer & Jones, 1972) provides a good set of guidelines that emphasize the following critical characteristics of a contract: *specificity, performance, involvement, realism,* and *observability.*

Specificity demands that your learning goals be specific rather than general or global. For instance, "To learn how to be a better social worker" is much too general, as is, "To learn how to respond to clients in a professional manner." An evaluation of what the student should be learning at any point in the academic term is facilitated by the more specific goal: "To learn how to screen clients for substance abuse."

By making your learning goals *performance* oriented, all three parties should have a good idea of the activities, duties, assignments, or responsibilities to be completed for you to meet your goals. For instance, it is generally necessary to interview clients in order to learn interviewing. Once the goal has been stated, it is desirable for objectives or tasks to be specified. For instance, a student who wants to learn how to conduct substance abuse evaluations might list below that goal the following objective: "To conduct at least ten substance abuse evaluations during the practicum placement."

Involvement ensures that the contract spells out the extent to which you, the field instructor, and the faculty field liaison will be involved in helping you to reach your learning goals. Obviously, if the field instructor and faculty field liaison approve of you learning how to screen for substance abuse, then you will have to be assigned enough clients for the objective to be achieved.

GEORGE GOODSTUDENT

Placement Agency: Rogers County Mental Health Services

Address: 1414 Evans Drive, Zanesville, Ohio

Phone: (513) 555–5000

Field Instructor: Mary Ann Mobbie, M.S.W.

Hours in Placement: Tuesday: 8:00 A.M. to 5:00 P.M.   Friday: 8:00 A.M. to 5:00 P.M.

Supervision Time: Tuesday: 8:30 A.M. to 10:00 A.M.

GOAL 1: TO IMPROVE INTERVIEWING SKILLS

Objective 1:   To read a book on interviewing during the 1st week (not on practicum time) and discuss any questions with the field instructor.

Objective 2:   To observe five interviews conducted by agency staff by the 2nd week.

Objective 3:   To videotape two interviews with clients by the end of the semester.

Objective 4:   To conduct at least 12 interviews with clients by the end of the semester.

GOAL 2: TO LEARN THE COMMUNITY'S SOCIAL SERVICES

Objective 1:   By midsemester to visit United Way's Information and Referral Center and interview two staff members about services available.

Objective 2:   To read 20 recently closed cases by the 7th week to identify referrals that were made.

Objective 3:   To attend at least five case conferences by the end of the semester.

GOAL 3: TO LEARN HOW TO CONDUCT GROUP THERAPY

Objective 1:   To observe for 3 weeks the incest survivors' support group.

Objective 2:   To attend the scheduled 4 hour in-service entitled "Working with Groups."

Objective 3:   To cofacilitate a new time-limited support group for male sexual abuse victims (8 weeks).

Student   _____   Date _____

Field Instructor   _____   Date _____

Faculty Field Liaison   _____   Date _____

Figure 3.1   Sample practicum learning contract

Your learning contract might also specify involvement in terms of visits the faculty field liaison will make to the agency or the supervision you will receive from your field instructor. (This makes the contract more than just a one-sided agreement.)

The element of *realism* is a reminder that your learning goals and associated objectives need to be realistic and attainable within the limits of the agency's educational resources, the time you will be in the practicum, and your personal assets and limitations.

Observability "demands that results be defined in a measurable form so that it is obvious whether or not the specific goal has been achieved" (Abbott, 1986, p. 61).

Although the absolute number of substance abuse screenings to be completed may not always be critical, it is important that an impartial observer be able to determine whether or not you have completed your objectives.

Try to strike a balance between ambitiousness and practicality in your learning contract. Discussion with your field instructor and faculty field liaison will help to identify areas where change or modification is needed.

Ideas for Enriching the Practicum Experience

1. Why was your agency originally created or funded? What was its mission statement at its inception? Has the agency's mission changed over the years? Try to find a copy of the agency's constitution, bylaws, or charter to read.
2. How well known is your agency? How often has your agency or its staff received newspaper coverage in the past year? Ask your friends, neighbors, or relatives what they know about the agency where you will be placed. If the agency has a unique logo or emblem, how many recognize it? How many know where the agency is located? If you feel that the agency does not have a high level of community recognition (based on your small sample), what could be done to make it more visible?
3. Determine whether or not a community resource or referral list exists in your agency. When was it updated last? Is it complete? Whose responsibility is it to keep the list current? If the list is in need of updating and you have the time, ask your field instructor if you can assist with this project.
4. Putting aside your learning contract for a moment, what skills will your current practicum offer you a chance to develop that will interest future employers? How would you describe these skills on a résumé? (If you do not feel that your practicum is providing you with any marketable skills, you need to discuss ways of enhancing this practicum with your faculty field liaison.)

References

Abbott, A. A. (1986). The field placement contract: Its use in maintaining comparability between employment-related and traditional field placements. *Journal of Social Work Education, 22*(1), 57–66.

Pfeiffer, J. W., & Jones, J. E. (1972). Criteria of effective goal-setting: The SPIRO model. In *The 1972 annual handbook for group facilitators.* La Jolla, CA: University Associates.

Additional Readings

Cohen, M. B. & Ruff, E. (1995). The use of role play in field instructor training. *Journal of Teaching in Social Work,* 11, 85–100.

Maluccio, A., & Marlow, W. D. (1974). The case for the contract. *Social Work, 19*(1), 28–36.

Seabury, B. (1976). The contract: Uses, abuses, and limitations. *Social Work, 21*(1), 16–21.

Chapter **4**

The Student Intern: Learning New Roles

Overview

Student interns may feel that they are hybrid creatures—treated sometimes like an employee, sometimes like a volunteer. It is easy to be confused about roles when one is sometimes allowed only to observe professional staff in action, and other times given enormous responsibilities. This chapter attempts to help the student understand the differences among volunteer, student, and employee roles.

What Are the Differences Among Volunteer, Student, and Employee Roles?

Every day, each of us assumes many roles. For instance, our behavior may reflect our status as a son or daughter, mother or father, student, employee, or volunteer. Social service agencies differ in how they view student interns, and their understanding of the internship role will determine what students will be given to do, the amount of supervision they will receive, and how their performance will be evaluated. Your own educational experience will be enriched by a clear understanding of the differences among the volunteer, student, and employee roles.

Depending on the agency, the differences between a volunteer and a student intern may be barely perceptible. For instance, both volunteer counselors and student interns at a rape crisis center may have to complete 40 hours of training and orientation before they have any client contact. In other settings, such as a psychiatric unit of a hospital, volunteers (e.g., candy stripers) have very different responsibilities from those of student interns.

Although students and volunteers might at times be given similar tasks, students have the additional responsibility of learning why a task was done, why it was done the way it was, and how that task relates to the larger picture of planned intervention. Being a student involves thinking, analyzing, and reflecting, as well as doing. Students are expected to see the connection between assessment, planning, and intervention. Students should feel that they may ask questions and ask for reference material in areas where they have little knowledge, and should be given the opportunity to observe and practice new skills.

Volunteers tend to be given mundane chores (e.g., addressing envelopes or answering the telephone) because they are seen as just "helping out." Such volunteer assignments generally do not require close supervision. Although you as a student may be given some of the same responsibilities as volunteers, these should make up only a small portion of your time in the practicum. If you find that the bulk of your practicum time is filled with tedious chores that do not allow you to grow intellectually as a social worker, then your agency may view you more as a volunteer than as a student.

As an intern, you ought to be working with clients, families, and groups directly (unless you are in certain administrative or research placements). You should have questions about what you are doing. Similarly, your field instructor should be interested in how you are doing and should want to know about the progress of your cases. Your direct, private supervision should be no less than one or two hours a week and should include suggestions from the field instructor regarding other approaches, strategies, and theories; perhaps including information about how the field instructor handled a similar situation (more on how to make the best use of supervision later in this chapter).

Unlike volunteers, who may work as much or little as pleases them, students have a specified number of practicum hours that must be spent in their assigned agencies. Both volunteers and students need their supervisors to agree to their proposed schedules before starting in the agency. Sometimes days and hours are negotiated—one day might be more convenient than another. This contrasts rather markedly with the employee who is told the days and exact hours to work. Employees may be given little choice in tasks or responsibilities to perform. Agencies expect more from employees than from students or volunteers in productivity and knowledge about their jobs. But then, of course, employees are generally rewarded financially for their trials and tribulations.

In some situations, clients accept volunteers more easily than they do students. One undergraduate volunteering in a mental hospital explained,

> The patients were more accepting of me when I was a volunteer because they believed I came to the hospital not because I had to, but because I cared and wanted to be with them. They saw students as being interested in them as subjects for research rather than as individual human beings.

Students placed in residential facilities may find that residents resent students who come into their lives and then leave abruptly at the end of the academic term.

Unlike employees and students, volunteers are seldom evaluated. Generally speaking, there are never enough volunteers in agencies, and even inept volunteers are often tolerated. Volunteers may be informed that their services are no longer needed if they are unreliable (e.g., they do not show up on the days expected or do not accomplish assigned tasks). Students, on the other hand, are usually formally evaluated at the midpoint and toward the end of their academic terms. Social work students' experience in the practicum is guided (and to some degree regulated) by their learning contracts, which specify educational goals and objectives. Faculty field liaisons ensure that meaningful learning is occurring and help troubleshoot any problems that develop.

Students sometimes feel that they are being treated as free labor. For instance, one student complained bitterly when she was asked (in a residential setting) to help with some of the housekeeping chores. However, all of the paid staff were expected to perform certain menial chores to keep the facility clean and neat. The student was not being asked to do anything that staff members themselves did not do. However, students should be concerned when most assignments seem to be more related to housekeeping than to professional responsibilities. If you think that you are being unjustly treated because you are a student, then you have a legitimate complaint that you should share with your field instructor. On the other hand, if you are being assigned what you consider an unpleasant chore or responsibility that other staff members also perform or take turns doing, then you probably have little reason to complain.

Case Example

Jim shows up for the first day of his practicum and finds that the agency is closed to clients. The whole agency is in a retreat because of a recent reorganization. He finds his faculty field instructor, who invites him to accompany her to a series of staff meetings. At times the discussion becomes heated. Junior staff members disagree with their supervisors. Jim does not think that this is proper and by noon is beginning to wonder if he has made a mistake in selecting this agency. By 3:00, however, things seem to have smoothed out and a genuine sense of camaraderie is evident. In fact, staff members have decided to come into the agency on Saturday, on their own time, to have a clean-up, fix-up day. Because their maintenance and improvement budget has been severely cut over the past three years, they intend to paint several offices on their own and to wash windows both inside and out.

Questions

1. Should Jim also volunteer to work on Saturday?
2. What would be the advantages of getting to know the staff members on an informal basis?
3. What if Jim already had plans to go out of town?
4. Should he feel that it is beneath his dignity to wash windows or paint?

Do Students Have the Same Privileges as Staff Members?

You may be abruptly reminded that you are a student, not an employee, when you arrive at the agency extra early some morning and find the doors locked. You can't get in because you don't have a key. Similarly, you may not be able to work late because you can't lock up. Although being an employee of an agency implies certain responsibilities, usually there are other perks that also go along.

For instance, the agency may recognize a holiday that your university does not. The employees will get that day off, but if it falls on a day that you are scheduled to be in the agency, you will have to make up that time. You may find that the secretary in the agency treats the work you ask to be typed with a lower priority than she does that of the regular employees.

Even though in other areas you feel like a part of the team, you may be caught off guard when an incident suddenly reminds you of your internship status. This might happen when a long-time employee is retiring and a group of employees decides to take this person to lunch. You might be asked to stay behind and answer the phones in their absence. Or your field instructor may not inform you about a planned agency-wide retreat or special staff meeting.

These minor affronts should be ignored, for the most part. It is helpful to remember that your role is of a student and others in the agency may have privileges that you do not. This does not mean that you are disliked, probably only that they view you, as a transient—which, in fact, you are. If, however, you feel that you have a contribution to make at the special staff meeting, or that attending the planned retreat can be justified educationally, then inform your field instructor that you would like to attend and ask if it would be appropriate for you to do so.

Above all else, do not become bitter or resentful if you do not have the same privileges as staff. Work hard, do your best, and keep a good attitude. These are the traits by which you want to be remembered—especially when you are applying for jobs or graduate school and need letters of reference.

What Do I Need to Know About Interdisciplinary Team Meetings?

Many students will have the opportunity to participate on interdisciplinary teams often found in hospitals, nursing homes, schools, rehabilitation centers, and prisons. As a rule, the student's role initially will be that of observer until the student has a case to present or is asked to become more involved by the field instructor or other team member. This will usually happen after the student has had occasion to work with or observe clients being discussed by the team.

The persons who make up interdisciplinary teams have their particular expertise and responsibilities. Team members share a common purpose as they meet to pool knowledge, ideas, and plans for intervention. Interdisciplinary teams offer a framework within which specialists can work together to provide services for the whole client.

Students need to understand the overall purpose of a particular team, who makes up the team, how membership is decided, and its agreed goals. The goals determine how often the team will meet and how it will reach and implement decisions. It is also helpful to know the backgrounds of the individual team members and their philosophies, roles, and attitudes. The pooling of members' unique perspectives allows for consideration of the problem from many different angles. These points of view justify each person's inclusion on the team.

If you are expected to be an active team member rather than an observer, do not be intimidated. You may have information not acquired by other professionals, or a better relationship with the client that has allowed new information to sift out. Especially if you have had an opportunity to see the client in a different capacity (e.g., with other clients or family members), your insights will be valued.

When you are not speaking, listen carefully to what each person is saying. Come prepared and be familiar with the cases that are to be discussed. As a social worker, facilitate communication, provide information useful for problem solving, and see that arrangements are made for any needed coordination of services.

How Much Will I Be Given to Do?

The amount of work assigned to students in practicum is not standardized. Students who possess more maturity, intelligence, competence, and prior experience will probably end up with larger caseloads than students who lack one or more of these traits. Even if you are easily the most mature person you know, some agencies may require you to spend the first semester observing and listening before being given the responsibility of staffing the crisis phone lines in the second semester.

In most agencies, a rough rule of thumb is that student interns might expect to carry four to seven cases at a time. Two or three cases are too few, and ten or more are often too many unless a student is in a block placement and working 30 hours or more a week in the agency. Four or five cases will keep a student reasonably occupied—especially if these have different diagnoses or distinctive problems that require background or additional reading.

It is true that four or five cases will not keep a student completely occupied if he or she is placed in an agency for 20 hours per week or so. At a minimum, students should expect to be involved in some type of professional activity at least half of the time. In addition to managing their own cases, students often can assist with client intake assessments, participate in case conferences or staff meetings, accompany other staff who make home visits, and observe group or family therapy sessions. By planning ahead, students might ask to participate in a particular type of session (e.g., termination with a client) that they will need to handle by themselves later in the academic term.

Since agencies vary markedly with regard to their clientele, some students may have few clients initially, but these are ongoing or long term; while students in other agencies may have many more clients over the academic term, but these involve briefer contacts. Actually, a combination of both short- and long-term clients would be ideal. Optimally, a student should receive clients at intake and keep them throughout the treatment process until the clients terminate services.

As a student, it is to your advantage to learn as much as possible about the agency and the way it serves its clientele. If you feel that you are being underutilized, talk with your field instructor. He or she may agree to your taking on other assignments within the agency. Perhaps you could assist with a small research or evaluation project. It may be possible, for instance, to contact former clients to determine if they require additional intervention from the agency. You could plan this sort of project whenever things are reasonably caught up and in between other scheduled clients or activities.

Another educationally meaningful activity is to update the agency's community resource directory. Most agencies maintain a file of health and human resources they use when referring clients. Often these files are loosely organized, with penciled notes and brochures that may not be current. By contacting some of these programs yourself and becoming familiar with these resources, you can learn what services are available, their eligibility requirements, and how they can be accessed by your clients.

Talk with your field instructor to find out if any agency personnel are engaged in such activities as planning and creating new resources. It is not uncommon for agency-based social workers to be involved with task forces, coalitions, or community planning groups that may be conducting needs assessments or trying to document the need for new programs in the community. Such groups may have special projects that could use your assistance.

Still another useful educational strategy is to interview staff with whom you have not worked. Ask them what they think is important to know to do their jobs well. Be assertive in meeting other staff members as you attempt to get more involved in the agency. If after these efforts you still feel that too much of your time is being wasted, then it is appropriate to inform your faculty field liaison. Problems you encounter during your field instruction are the mutual responsibility of three parties: the faculty field liaison, the field instructor, and you. All three must be involved to ensure the integrity of the field instruction.

If you feel that you are being treated more like a staff than a student and given too much responsibility for the time you are in the agency, you'll probably begin to feel stressed. If you are hard-pressed to complete your paperwork or assignments on time, if you are tense and feeling too much pressure, you may have to learn how to say "no" nicely—by pointing out that you are only a student. It is important that you learn how to advocate for yourself, if you are to be an effective advocate for your clients. However, if demands upon you from the agency do not let up, you will need to speak to your faculty field liaison.

Case Example

Eileen decided to return to college after her children finished high school. At 45, she is the oldest student in her integrating seminar. Because of her maturity and good judgment, Eileen is placed in a very active social work department in a large metropolitan hospital. Very soon after her orientation, she is treated as a regular staff member—possibly because of an unfilled vacancy and the pregnancy leave of another social worker. Eileen is kept so busy on her practicum that she is often too busy to reflect or discuss with her agency supervisor what she has learned at the end of the day. On average, Eileen is working one or two hours extra each day she is in her practicum.

Usually, although not always, Eileen and her agency supervisor are able to find an hour once a week to talk. Eileen is beginning to resent having so much responsibility and so little time to study, read, and reflect as some of her classmates are finding time to do. Her supervisor has hinted that she knows Eileen is being given too much to do, but they are going to be shorthanded for at least another four weeks. And, there is the possibility of a permanent job opening up for Eileen even while she is going to school. Eileen is torn between wanting to be considered for the vacant position and wanting to be treated as a student and not given quite so much responsibility.

Questions

1. Should Eileen have a "showdown" with her supervisor and complain about being overworked?
2. Does Eileen need to involve her faculty field liaison?

3. Could Eileen be a good intern and still cut back on her hours?
4. How would you cope in such a situation?
5. How do you cope with stress?

How Much Will I Be Supervised, and by Whom?

A qualified social work supervisor (field instructor) should be regularly accessible within the agency where you are placed. If your immediate agency supervisor does not hold a social work degree, then another person with social work credentials may be asked to provide your formal or official supervision at least once a week. In a few instances where a program or agency does not employ any social workers but where a rich learning opportunity is available, a social work faculty member may be asked to provide your supervision.

Your agency supervisor will be responsible for giving you duties or assignments and monitoring your performance. He or she will be in charge of you, and unless you are informed to the contrary, this is the person to whom you should turn if you have any questions or problems while carrying out your assignments.

A major difference between the type of supervision you will receive as a student and other nonprofessional supervision that you may have experienced in paid employment or voluntary jobs is that the field instructor has a major teaching role. Field instructors attempt to introduce students to a wide range of activities performed by social workers. In keeping with their teaching role, they may also assign readings to assist students in better understanding their clients or improving certain skills. Practicum experience is designed to help students learn specific social work skills and knowledge in accordance with their learning contracts.

From an agency's perspective, students require supervision (sometimes very close supervision), which takes away from the field instructor's own productivity—unless the students' contributions offset the investment of time. Field instructors will be relieved when you can be a help, but until you demonstrate that you can handle certain tasks, expect your supervisor to keep a careful watch over you. Gradually, as you demonstrate your competence and the two of you get to know each other more, supervision will become more relaxed. Students who require too much supervision and those who cannot be trusted with even the smallest of assignments may be asked to leave.

Most often, field instructors will be cautious not to give students any assignments that would exceed their level of expertise. The initial tasks may be fairly elementary. Agency supervisors will gauge students' handling of these tasks before giving them more advanced or demanding assignments. If your work is sloppy and careless, there will be little reason to give you more responsibility or more complex assignments. Similarly, if you take too long or fail to complete your assignments, you will not be perceived as a resource or an asset to the agency, but as a liability.

In our experience, the amount of time allotted for supervisory conferences changes as the semester progresses. Generally, supervisors spend more time with students at the beginning of the placement than when students are past the first several weeks of orientation. Field instructors want to get students off to a good start and want to be sure that students understand agency policy and procedure. Once students are involved and doing well, supervisors may not be so deliberate or constant in monitoring how they are doing.

Because students seem to do better when supervision is consistent and predictable, we recommend that you set a specific time each week with the field instructor to ensure that supervision occurs. If this detail was overlooked in your learning contract, do not let several weeks go by without at least one hour of supervision. Do not settle for five minutes here and ten minutes there. The quality of supervision provided on the run is not the same as when both of you have time to think about what you have been learning and what you still need to learn.

How Do I Make Supervision Work for Me?

Getting the most out of supervision requires that you know what supervision is, what the dynamics of the supervisory relationship are, and what specific actions facilitate effective supervision.

Supervisors oversee the work of others. Supervisors administer and coordinate; they provide consultation to help their supervisees perform more effectively and efficiently. Supervisors explain important agency policies and procedures, provide on-the-job training, assess performance, and make suggestions for improvement. In addition, supervisors participate in the hiring and firing of employees, mediate problems between their subordinates and the agency, and sometimes fill in for employees who are sick or absent. They are repositories of knowledge about the agency and the clientele. Above all else, supervisors are responsible for seeing that clients are provided quality services.

Interesting dynamics are generated in the process of supervision. From the subordinate's perspective, some supervisors are not good teachers. They may not know how to correct gently or how to make a suggestion without it sounding like criticism. Unfortunately, these supervisors can hurt feelings without intending to do so. A former student once reported that her supervisor thought that she "had to be critical" or else the student would not think that she had a knowledgeable field instructor.

From the supervisor's perspective, some individuals clearly resent having a boss who tells them what to do. Supervisors have a difficult time overseeing individuals who are irritated at the very thought of having to account for their activities and who may find passive-aggressive ways to sabotage a supervisory relationship (e.g., showing up late for supervision, or "forgetting" about a supervisory conference and scheduling a client at the same time).

Some nontraditional social work students have had managerial experience in other careers before deciding to become social workers. It may be difficult in such situations to accept the fact that, although they may be peers in age or in other life experiences, the subordinate-supervisor relationship is not a peer or reciprocal relationship.

The time that you spend with your agency supervisor should be an opportunity for you to grow professionally, by availing yourself of the supervisor's practice experience and knowledge. If you are feeling overwhelmed or confused, supervisors can help you to rank your tasks so that the most important ones are completed first. If you do not know how to do your assigned jobs, your supervisor can provide direction as to what to do, how to do it, and when.

A good supervisor should reduce your anxiety and increase your sense of competence and self-worth by listening to you and being concerned when you have problems. He or she should be a successful problem solver who follows through with commitments. Hopefully, your supervisor will tell you when you are doing something right, as well as explain when you are doing something unacceptable.

You can get the most out of your supervisory conferences by planning for them. Before a scheduled conference, write down a list of questions you have, problems you want to discuss, or observations you want to make. Be prepared to inform your agency supervisor what assignments you have accomplished and which are nearing completion. Be able to account for how you have spent your time. If you are not being given enough to do, ask for new assignments or additional responsibilities.

Should you have a client who is making no progress or who is a difficult case, then take advantage of the time with your agency supervisor to discuss it. There may be other ways to view the problem, or alternative treatment strategies or resources—or the situation may be too complex for a student to handle. We all learn from our mistakes. Do not be afraid to be completely honest with your agency supervisor. For instance, assume that you unthinkingly used a poor choice of words which caused Mrs. Jones to storm off in anger. You feel that it is your fault and that the client may never return to the agency. By sharing this with your supervisor, you may learn that Mrs. Jones is irascible and in the past has stomped off in anger on the average of once a month or so. Instead of being worried (and maybe guilty) about offending Mrs. Jones, sharing this information may help you to learn more about Mrs. Jones's personality and level of functioning.

Supervision can help you to develop professionally—but only if you want to learn from it. Ask questions about things you want to know. Ask for articles or books that would help you to understand the cases you are handling. Be active in learning from your supervisor. Reflect on the feedback you have been given.

What is the Purpose of Field Seminars?

As a part of the practicum requirements, many social work programs require students to participate in weekly seminars. A *seminar* is a small group of students engaged in a special study under the guidance of a professor. The basic assumption underpinning seminars is that each person in attendance has important information to share or contribute. By contrast, in lecture courses the assumption is that the professor has the most knowledge and will be the prime communicator of ideas.

Usually, field seminars are conducted by faculty field liaisons, although they may be directed by field instructors or even students themselves. Faculty field liaisons or seminar leaders make arrangements for the time and place of the meeting, and they determine the frequency of the seminars as well as the focus of each session. In addition, it is their responsibility to see that the discussions are relevant to students' current experiences in their practicum placements. Many see their seminar leadership role as helping students (1) to understand their cases in terms of applicable theories, and (2) to integrate discoveries in an area (e.g., practice) with content from another (e.g., policy or research implications).

Seminars may be highly structured, as when students are given specific reading assignments or are asked to make presentations. Or seminars may be loosely structured, as when students take turns relating significant experiences or problems that recently occurred in the field. In structured seminars, it is likely that the faculty field liaison will choose the topics and carefully focus student discussion. Similarly, the faculty field liaison may give specific directions for seminar presentations. Here are a few suggestions if you are required to make a presentation:

1. Keep within the time limit (organize your thoughts and rehearse your presentation).
2. Begin with a brief introduction of what you intend to cover.
3. Limit your main points to three or four and support these with illustrations.
4. Summarize your main points at the end of your presentation.
5. Stimulate discussion by looking at each person as you speak.
6. Use visual aids to clarify ideas.
7. Anticipate questions, and to encourage discussion, ask several questions of your own.

Whether their seminars are structured or unstructured, most faculty field liaisons prefer that all students contribute to seminar discussions. Informal exchanges can help to increase comfort with the way intervention is proceeding. Learning that your peers have had similar experiences or even that they would have handled the problem the same way you did can be very reassuring. In the best seminars, students can feel free to raise questions with the faculty member or other students—to ask for resources or help with a special situation or problem.

To get the most out of an unstructured seminar, prepare ahead of time by reflecting on the past week's important events. Rank order these when time is limited, so that the most pressing matters can be discussed first. Try not to monopolize the group's time. In some instances, it may be necessary to continue the discussion with your faculty field liaison after the seminar or to make an appointment for this purpose.

In seminars, you are expected to be a good listener when others are speaking, to stay alert, and to interact with others in the group. A seminar works well only when everyone takes part of the responsibility to make it interesting by raising questions and sharing information that may not be common knowledge.

How Will My Faculty Field Liaison Evaluate Me?

We cannot inform you of exactly what your faculty field liaison will personally expect of you. However, you can get some idea of these expectations from the syllabus and from the instructor's presentation at the first class meeting (or at the time you received your syllabus or field manual). This is the time to ask questions if you want to know more about how you will be evaluated.

On the basis of our own experiences supervising students in the field and our contacts with other faculty field liaisons, we can talk generally about what faculty field liaisons expect of students. To understand this perspective, you must keep in mind that although faculty field liaisons are concerned with what you are learning and your performance in the agency, they are at the disadvantage of not seeing very much (if any) of your work in the agency. Because they have the responsibility of assigning a grade to your efforts, they need feedback from your agency supervisor and possibly such evidence as they can collect from assignments. Some faculty field liaisons allow written assignments to carry more weight than evaluations from agency supervisors. These faculty field liaisons typically expect that all assignments will be completed on time, that any field logs or process recordings will be kept current, and that you show up for scheduled appointments to discuss the placement. If your grade is more dependent on written assignments than on agency input, then you may earn a lower grade than you think you deserve, even if you are doing superior work in the agency.

Grading schemes are often somewhat subjective. One faculty field liaison may let the course grade be largely determined by the agency supervisor's recommendation; another may weigh written assignments or case presentations more heavily; a third may penalize you for missing seminars or classes; and a fourth may pass everyone as long as no problems occurred in the agency. Your course syllabus should state specifically how your grade will be determined. Many programs use a pass/fail method, which seems to take pressure off grades.

You can avoid failing or unsatisfactory grades, as a rule, by following the syllabus and using common sense. Beyond this, conventional wisdom would tell you to avoid asking for exceptions to existing policy or rules. The following true illustrations are provided to help you understand what faculty field liaisons *do not* want in their students.

> Nancy decided about halfway through the semester that she did not like her practicum supervisor. Without telling anyone, she went into the agency on a Sunday morning and cleaned out her desk. When she didn't show on Monday or Tuesday, the supervisor called the faculty field liaison to see if Nancy was ill.

A more responsible student would have informed the faculty field liaison of perceived problems in the agency and would have allowed the faculty field liaison time to investigate and work out either a new field instructor, new responsibilities, or a new practicum.

> Susan missed the first three meetings of her required weekly practicum seminar. It was necessary, she said, because she needed to work and as a result had to schedule practicum clients at the same time as the seminar. She could not understand why her faculty field liaison was unhappy with her lack of attendance. "After all," she said, "the agency staff are pleased with me."

> Rob managed to delight agency staff with his good humor and ability to work with children, but somehow he never found time to write his logs or document the number of hours he spent in the agency. His paperwork for his faculty field liaison was late by several weeks on each occasion that it was due.

Faced with situations such as these, it is easy to see how some students will distinguish themselves as being conscientious ("A") students and others will fall short of that mark. Neither agencies nor faculty field liaisons expect you to have supernatural abilities in order to succeed. Usually, success comes about through attention to details, such as completing assignments in a timely fashion, conforming to the expectations of the syllabus, showing up when expected in the agency, and displaying common courtesy.

Some practicum instructors use an evaluation form devised by Wilson (1981). She lists 20 professional/personal characteristics on which a student can be evaluated using behavioral expectations. (See Box 4.1.) Consider, for example, the characteristic she calls "Professional Responsibility." Students can be measured on this behavior along a contin-

Box 4.1   Wilson's List of Twenty Professional/Personal Characteristics

Professional Responsibility
Poise and Self-Control
Assertiveness
Personal Appearance as Related to Agency Standards
Effectiveness in Planning and Arranging Work Responsibilities
Ability to Assume Responsibility for Own Learning
Ability to Work Within the Purpose, Structure, and Constraints of the
    Agency and to Make Suggestions for Change in a Responsible Manner
Ability to Identify and Use Community Resources
Interviewing Skills, Including the Ability to Recognize and Interpret the
    Meaning of Nonverbal Communication
Written Communication Skills, Including the Ability to Record with Clarity
    and Promptness
Ability to Assess Situations Both Within and Outside the Client System and
    Determine Priorities
Ability to Develop and Maintain Professional Relationships with Consumers
    from Various Cultural, Ethnic, and Racial Backgrounds
Relationship with Coworkers (Other Students in the Agency as Well as
    Agency Staff)
Relationship with Staff of Other Agencies
Demonstration of the Acceptance and Use of Basic Social Work Values,
    Ethics, and Principles
Effectiveness in Providing Services to Individuals and Families
Effectiveness in Providing Services to Small Groups
Effectiveness in Providing Services at the Community Level
Use of Supervision
Development of a Professional Self-Awareness, Including the Need for
    Continued Professional Growth

uum. A student functioning at the "A" level is "consistently responsible about all aspects of work and makes excellent use of time." An "F" student "appears bored with his work and puts self-interests first. Has a pattern of tardiness and/or absenteeism."

Your faculty field liaison may use this or some other scheme to evaluate your performance in the agency. Urbanowski and Dwyer (1988), for instance, have conceptualized criteria for field practice performance that vary slightly depending on whether the student is graduate or undergraduate, and if undergraduate, first or second semester. A sampling of these items is as follows:

First Semester Undergraduate
Functioning within the agency and community. The student begins to understand the structural components of the agency and has developed a good roster of social agency resources that would be helpful to clients.

Second Semester Undergraduate
Functioning within the agency and community. The student has comfort with the more commonly used policies and procedures and has the ability to interpret them clearly to clients and the community. The student organizes assignments so that maximum services are provided for all clients. Shows concern about obvious community problems.

First Semester Graduate
Functioning within the agency and community. The student knows the structure and function of the agency, and understands the administrative hierarchy and the process of decision making at the local agency level. The student can make connections between the agency goals, policies, and procedures, and the services offered to clients. The student implements these services in accordance with the needs of the client and is aware of the inherent inequities in the overall social service system for special groups.

Second Semester Graduate
Functioning within the agency and community. The student assumes responsibility for continual learning about the agency and for creatively using the resources within it. The student has a solid knowledge about the operations of surrounding social systems and knows how to use these systems for the welfare of clients. The student is sensitive to the violation of clients' rights and explores action to remedy such situations.

How Do I Juggle All My Roles Simultaneously?

During the course of a semester, many students experience anxiety from having to juggle too many roles and demands simultaneously. Studying and family responsibilities may conflict with work obligations, often causing a no-win situation. Whatever obligations they choose to meet, these pressured students may feel stress or guilt from omitting other, equally important obligations.

What can you do to reduce the problems caused by role conflicts? A good starting place is to consider your priorities. For example, if you are a parent, you will probably decide that the needs of your children have to come first. Taking care of sick children, preparing their meals, and finding time for them may be more important than getting all A's. Likewise, you may have to learn how to let some household chores slide for a day or two so you can study for an exam. "Something is going to have to give," one married undergraduate said, "I just can't do everything that I used to."

People who are well organized find it easier to juggle the additional roles of being a student and a practicum intern. You can assess your own level of organization. Disorganization may be suggested whenever you:

- Have frequent feelings of being behind and not caught up
- Procrastinate so long on an assignment that it becomes an emergency or panic situation
- Miss a deadline

- Misplace necessities such as car keys, glasses, or purse
- Have forgotten scheduled appointments, meetings, birthdays, or specific dates you wanted to remember
- Take more than ten minutes to unearth a particular letter, bill, or report from your files (or from the piles of paper on your desk)
- Are surprised at the end of most days by how little you have been able to accomplish.

If you identify with two or more of these items, then you may need help in developing organizational skills. Three items are usually essential for better organization: a day-by-day calendar, a pocket-sized notebook, and a daily to-do list. Use the calendar to record all appointments, deadlines, and crucial events. In your notebook, jot down errands and tasks you need to do as they occur to you. Think about your long- and short-term goals. Place on your to-do list and on your calendar the things that must be done in order for you to accomplish your goals. The to-do list should be compiled every day and should contain no more than ten specific items. Rank order the items so that the most important are completed first.

Here are a few other suggestions for getting the most out of the time available to you: Find a few minutes each day so you can plan. When you think about tomorrow, prepare to do the most difficult tasks first and at a time when you will be free from interruptions and can concentrate most effectively. Recently, a student attending a social work convention asked the director of a large agency how he was able to supervise more than 80 employees. He replied that he came into the office at 6:30 every morning because he was able to get more paperwork and planning done between then and 8:30 than throughout the rest of the entire day. He purposefully looked for a quiet time in the agency and then put it to his full use.

Limit the number of outside activities that drain away your time while you are a student intern. Carefully consider requests being made of you. If you almost always say yes to additional projects or responsibilities outside of the practicum, try imposing a temporary moratorium. If it is difficult to refuse new requests, give yourself some time to think about them. If after you have done so you decide that it is not in your best interest to help, call and explain this. Keep your response simple and to the point. Inform others that you would like to help but simply do not have the time.

Try to avoid insignificant activities that clutter your life and distract you—for example, watching soap operas or game shows on television while preparing for classes the next day.

Break large tasks into smaller segments. This will make the job seem much more manageable and will help you to avoid procrastination. For instance, if you have a 20-page term paper to write, plan to go to the library on Sunday to gather your resources. Create the outline for your paper on Monday. On Tuesday, write the introduction to the paper, and continue in this way to divide up the major task.

One final thought about juggling many roles: This situation can be viewed negatively or positively. On one hand, it could be seen as an "impossible" situation destined to create difficulties. On the other hand, it could be seen as an opportunity to develop better organizational skills while engaged in learning how to be a social worker. Having many commitments can actually work to your advantage by structuring your time. One graduate student explained,

> When I have time available for studying, I don't waste a minute! I never put things off any more because I can't predict when one of my children might get sick or when my boss might ask me to work extra hours. Being a mother and an employee has actually helped me to prioritize my activities and to get the most out of the hours in my day.

How Do I Know if I'm Stressed Out?

Despite good organizational skills, planning, and wise use of available time, most students occasionally experience high stress. Individuals react uniquely to stress, but here are some common symptoms:

- Inability to sleep
- Irritability
- Feeling pressured or "smothered"
- Headaches and stomachaches
- Weight loss or gain
- Being tearful or more emotional
- Being unable to concentrate or focus on a task

How Can I Effectively Manage the Stress in My Life?

Stress is not all bad. It can motivate you to get things done. However, too much stress can immobilize. When you sense you are approaching the limits of your ability to handle the stresses in your life, think about how you relax. What helps you to deal with stress? Here are some common ways to reduce daily stress:

- Engage in some type of exercise (even walking)
- Do something enjoyable (go to a movie, start a novel, work in a garden or on a favorite hobby)
- Have a conversation with a close friend
- Play a musical instrument or listen to music
- Take a short nap
- Do deep-breathing, relaxation exercises
- Examine any recurrent thoughts for irrational, perfectionistic beliefs
- Make a plan, enlist some help
- Try to find some humor in your situation

If you are feeling highly stressed, bring the subject up in your seminar and see if other students are feeling the same way. You may be surprised to learn that others are feeling just as stressed as you are. This group can serve in some ways as a support group for you. Also, it may assist you by suggesting resources or providing information that could help with a problematic client or situation. If, however, you have followed just about all of the suggestions provided here and you still have such a high level of stress that it is presenting problems for you, then it is time to seek a competent professional for assistance. Your field instructor or faculty field liaison may suggest that you contact your university counseling center or suggest professionals in the community.

The Student Intern's "Bill of Rights"

Sometimes when you are new to a situation it is hard to know whether your experiences are unique, or similar to the experiences of others. Being a student intern differs from being a student in the classroom, and the newness of the internship experience and the responsibilities given to you may be almost overwhelming at times. If you are feeling this way, you may not be getting enough supervision from your field instructor. To give you some basis for reality checking, Munson (1987) has drafted a set of rights to which practicum students are entitled:

1. The right to a field instructor who supervises them consistently at regularly designated times.
2. The right to a sufficient number and variety of cases to ensure learning.
3. The right to growth-oriented, as well as technical and theoretical, learning that is stable in its expectations.
4. The right to clear criteria for performance evaluation.
5. The right to a field instructor who is adequately trained and skilled in supervision. (pp. 105–106)

If you feel that your "rights" are being overlooked or violated, then discuss this matter with your faculty field liaison. On many occasions, faculty intervention can help to clarify responsibilities and smooth things out. And when necessary, it is the faculty field liaison's role to advocate for a student and to ensure that the student is not being mistreated, being given poor supervision, or ignored. Do not be afraid to consult with your faculty field liaison when your intuition or best judgment tells you that things are not right with your supervision or treatment in the agency. In the event that your faculty field liaison is the problem, discuss your difficulties with your academic adviser or the chairperson or academic head of your social work program.

Myths You Can Do Without

One of the refreshing aspects of working with students is their idealism. There's something quite wonderful about the energy and enthusiasm that students bring, their interest in trying to make the world a better place. However, the "School of Hard Knocks" sometimes forces students to adjust erroneous assumptions after a painful lesson. We've listed some myths that we've discarded over our careers. You might want to do a little self-examination to see if you, too, might be stereotyping or over-idealizing—it just might save you some disappointment and grief.

Nine statements that are *not* realistic:

- All social workers love their jobs
- All social workers are conscientious, ethical, trustworthy individuals
- Social workers always do what is in the client's best interest
- Organizations are always concerned about waste, inefficiency, or inept, marginally productive employees
- Clients will always like you
- Clients will keep most, if not all, of their appointments
- Every problem can be solved
- The primary responsibility for healing/curing clients rests in your hands
- Every client wants to get better

This is not to say that social work is a career filled with sleazy, unprincipled professionals or that clients won't astound you with their courage as they battle to change their lives and improve conditions for their children and loved ones. However, don't fall into the snare of romanticizing clients or expecting all social workers to be paragons of virtue. If you are lucky, you will find one or more mentors, solid, competent social workers, who will, by their example and instruction, help you to form reasonable and sensible expectations about those with whom you will be working. While you don't need to be cynical about everyone, you also don't need to be so quixotic as to overlook galloping self-interest and other less than flattering motivations underlying human behavior.

Ideas for Enriching the Practicum Experience

1. If you have blocks of unscheduled time in your agency, ask if you can visit other departments within the agency to learn what they do and about their clientele. Are there different eligibility considerations? Are there different fee schedules? Do the social workers in other departments have larger or smaller caseloads than those in the program where you have been assigned? How do their jobs vary?
2. If the agency where you have been assigned has volunteers, try to talk with several over lunch or during a break to learn about their contributions to the agency. Would services to clients be significantly affected if volunteers were not used? Considering the number of volunteers and the hours they contribute, what do you think is the value of their services? Are there other areas where volunteers could be used?
3. If there is a staff handbook or manual, read it as part of your orientation. Are there areas where the handbook is incomplete or needs to be expanded? Is there language to clarify the role of students? Are students treated more as nonpaid staff or as nonpaid volunteers?
4. Compare the evaluation form with which you will be evaluated with other examples that you can find (e.g., the personnel evaluation form used in the agency). Which form is the more comprehensive? From your reading of the evaluation

form that your field instructor and faculty field liaison will use, is it clear over what areas you will be evaluated?

5. Is supervision a new experience for you? If so, what does it feel like? Has your field instructor identified any special skills or strengths that you did not know you possessed? Keep a log of your feelings and the insights you acquire from sessions with your supervisor.

References

Munson, C. E. (1987). Field instruction in social work education. *Journal of Teaching in Social Work, 1*(1), 91–109.

Urbanowski, M. L., & Dwyer, M. M. (1988). *Learning through field instruction: A guide for teachers and students.* Milwaukee: Family Service America.

Wilson, S. (1981). *Field instruction: Techniques for supervisors.* New York: Free Press.

Additional Readings

Abbott, A. (1986). The field placement contract. *Journal of Social Work Education, 22*(1), 57–66.

Johnson, H. W. (1988). Volunteer work in the introductory course: A special curriculum component. *Journal of Social Work Education, 24*(2), 145–150.

Randolf, J. L. (1982). The rights and responsibilities of clientele in field instruction. In B. W. Sheafor & L. E. Jenkins (Eds.), *Quality field instruction in social work.* White Plains, NY: Longman.

Reamer, F. G. (1989). Liability issues in social work supervision. *Social Work, 34*(5), 445–448.

Chapter **5**

Client Systems: The Recipients of Service

Overview

Many social work students have never been required to ask for professional assistance or exposed to persons remarkably poor, or different from their own families of origin. Questions arise about how best to communicate and work with individuals, families, and communities who are unfamiliar. This chapter seeks to provide help for students in understanding and working with new client systems.

Who Are Clients?

If there were no problems, crises, difficulties, or requests for help in the world, then social workers would have no clients. Of primary concern to us is the client system, that is, the person or persons to whom our services are provided. Client systems may be individuals, families, small groups, organizations, or communities. Ideally, you will have opportunities to work with client systems of various sizes in your practicum experiences.

What is it Like to Be a Client?

Have you ever had a flat tire on a country road and then discovered that your spare was gone or that you had no jack? What would it be like to be in a strange city and accidentally lock your car keys inside your car? Would you be comfortable stopping a complete stranger and asking for assistance? People who are accustomed to having such things as savings accounts, family members and friends willing to help, and a good credit rating sometimes find it difficult to imagine not having any of these resources.

In an effort to help new students to become more empathic with the problems of the homeless, one seminary took students to a nearby city and gave them just enough money to make one phone call in case of an emergency. The students were instructed to learn about the city's social services by being homeless for 48 hours. Imagine how you would feel in such a situation. If it were an unfamiliar city and you were without a car or money, what emotions would you have? Would you know where to go? Would you feel overwhelmed? Bewildered? Lost? Fearful?

We can assume that most clients are experiencing significant problems and stress when they come into our public service agencies. They want help with their problems and relief from the stress that they are experiencing. Many clients have never had to ask for assistance from anyone before, and they may not know what kinds of help are available or whether they might qualify.

Other clients have made use of agency services before and may know the rules and procedures better than you do. They may be impatient, demanding, or even rude. Their frustration may come from having to deal with impersonal bureaucrats, completing long application forms, or living on the barest minimum of economic assistance in a decaying and dangerous neighborhood. Court-ordered or involuntary clients may have many sources of frustration in their lives and their anger can be compounded and turned against themselves or others if they don't ask for help. They may also appear anxious, self-destructive, or apathetic.

We all react differently to stress, and clients are much like us, but often without our resources. Some clients may view themselves as failures because of their problems. They may feel ashamed or bewildered—as when a tragic and unexpected situation has occurred. Take, for example, the woman who has just learned that her child has been sexually abused by her live-in partner. Imagine the range of emotions that the mother must feel—anger at the perpetrator, grief over the violation of the child and possible loss of an adult relationship, and guilt from not having been able to prevent the abuse. To these feelings we can add confusion over the best course of action (e.g., prosecution), and fear that the child has been permanently damaged or scarred.

When enough stress is heaped on some clients, they may break down and psychologically surrender. Many clients express a sense of being overwhelmed. They may become depressed, isolate themselves, and require help with problem-solving strategies. Certain clients will try to ignore or deny their problems and muddle through. Occasionally there are self-referred or voluntary clients who, after hesitating months or years, enter therapy with a great sense of urgency. For them, nothing can be done fast enough; they may pressure you to see them two or more times a week. In contrast, clients who are involuntary (because they have been mandated to seek help by a judge or officer of the court) may be hostile and uncooperative.

As a social work student in a practicum, you must accept each client as a unique human being who has immeasurable worth and dignity. You must understand the client's unique set of problems as the client experiences them. This entails being nonjudgmental and accepting of individual differences. Even if the client's problems are of his or her own making, you must realize that the client has needs that are not being met, and implement a plan to make the client more healthy or whole.

Occasionally, clients' problems will be so complex and convoluted that you will feel overwhelmed and inadequate. Even "simple" cases given to a student may later be found to be much more complicated than the presenting problem indicated. At any time that you feel inundated and unsure how to proceed, you should discuss this client with your agency supervisor.

Printed with the permssion of Chris Rosenthal.

What Do Clients Expect from Me?

One of the joys (and sometimes one of the frustrations) of social work is that the profession exposes practitioners to many different types of people. Social work clients may be well educated and sophisticated, or have little education and be ill informed about what happens during the helping process. For instance, one client was overheard telling a friend that nothing happened during the 50-minute counseling session; she added, "All we did was talk."

Some clients are so limited in their ability to articulate family or individual dysfunctioning that they express their problems in terms of having "bad nerves." In their minds, complex problems can be solved with a prescription. As a result, they may request or even expect the social worker to provide physical relief of these symptoms by helping them to obtain a prescription for medication. Even if they do not expect pills, clients may anticipate rapid relief from the difficulties that brought them to the agency.

Clients completely unfamiliar with the process of counseling may be confused or may misunderstand the purpose of the social worker's questions. It may be necessary to inform them that social workers help clients by talking with them to discover more about their problems and strengths. However, the social worker cannot merely tell clients that intervention will consist mostly of talking; he or she may need to elaborate or provide concrete examples. Consumers of social work interventions may expect the social worker to do most of the talking and to *tell* them what to do or how to change their lives. They may not understand that social workers do not give this kind of advice.

Clients with a little more sophistication may expect that social workers will conduct the intervention by talking, but they may have unrealistic expectations—hoping that all the problems in their household will be resolved within three or four weeks. Because a social worker helped a friend, neighbor, or relative with a specific problem in a brief period of time, some clients may envision a "cure" in the same amount of time—not realizing the difficulty in making comparisons with others.

Using your knowledge of human nature, you can anticipate all of the following:

1. Clients want to be treated as individuals and helped with their problems. Although not all clients expect immediate improvement in their life situations, most do not have the patience to wait months for the first signs of progress. Communicate some sense of hope that things will improve, but avoid making any promises that all of their problems will be resolved. Similarly, it is unwise to give specific dates by which clients can expect improvement.

2. Clients do not want to be inconvenienced. Usually, they want the initial interview to be scheduled without delay. They want the social worker to meet with them at convenient times, and they resent being kept waiting. Furthermore, they want the intervention to be as inexpensive as possible.

3. Clients may be unaccustomed to talking about personal problems. They may have never told any other person about their feelings, hopes or dreams, sexual difficulties, or the mental illness within their families. During the helping process, you will be encouraging the client to learn not only that such topics can be discussed without embarrassment or crudity, but also that expressing painful feelings in a therapeutic environment brings about progress.

4. Clients expect you to be the authority—to guide the conversations, to ask the questions, and to act as if you are in charge. If you are too indecisive, then clients will perceive a lack of competence. Clients expect you to have better information about how to solve their problems than they have. They may also expect you to have specialized knowledge that you do not have. Often it is appropriate to tell the client that you do not have certain information. On other occasions, you may feel more comfortable telling the client that you will attempt to find the necessary information and will have it available at your next session. Do not allow clients to force you into the role of advice giver. Clients must make their own choices.

5. Clients expect to be able to tell their problems to a sympathetic professional who will be sincere in trying to help them while protecting their confidentiality. Listen attentively to each client. Do not stereotype clients or make hurried judgments. Treat every client as you would want to be treated.

Case Example

The intake secretary motions for you to come over to her desk one afternoon. In a hushed voice she tells you to expect a client tomorrow who is going to be "angry, demanding, and obnoxious." Although you know that clients are not always going to be pleasant and enjoyable to work with, several times that afternoon your mind goes back to what the secretary said. In preparation, you pull Mrs. Havolec's case record and read it. She has been a client on at least four occasions—always presenting a different problem and always terminating on her own against professional advice. Usually she stops coming to the agency when it appears she may be on the verge of making some significant progress. She is a chronic client, and there are ample notes attesting to her being grouchy and quick tempered. Your reading of her record also uncovers that she seems to be the most ill-humored with the receptionist and that she becomes more agreeable and congenial when she interacts with persons of greater authority and status. You wonder whether you should bend the agency's policy and not inform Mrs. Havolec tomorrow that you are a student.

Questions

1. In the interest of getting along better with the client, would it be okay to wait a couple of sessions or so to inform Mrs. Havolec that you are a student?
2. What would you do if Mrs. Havolec demanded (after spending 15 minutes with you) to be transferred to another worker?
3. Would you feel comfortable asking her to give you a fair chance—to wait at least another 45 minutes or so before deciding she had to have another worker?

Should I Inform Clients that I Am a Student?

In a 1990–1991 survey of social service agencies where BSW and MSW students were placed for field instruction (Miller & Rodwell, 1997), 51% of the administrators and field supervisors indicated that students were instructed to identify themselves as students. Additionally, another 20% of the respondents said that instructions varied by individual field instructors, and 18% said that students were told to use their own judgment. Although the data are a bit dated, the bulk of agencies (and probably even more do now) seem to require students to inform clients about their being professionals in training.

Several authors have discussed the issue of informing clients about student status. Feiner and Couch (1985), for example, have considered many of the arguments for not informing clients but conclude that eliminating any secrecy about student status serves the profession better. Hepworth and Larsen (1990) support the position taken by Germain and Gitterman (1980) that students have an ethical responsibility to disclose their role to clients. Arguments for informing clients include these: Disclosure allows the student to be fully authentic in the relationship, and it will prevent problems later on during termination. Furthermore, it might be hard to keep this information from clients (e.g., clients may call when students are not in the agency, and the receptionist might reply that they are unavailable but will be back from school by noon). Also, concealing one's student status might cause problems for the agency if a serious problem occurred (e.g., the client commits suicide) and the surviving family was looking for grounds to go to court.

In at least one state, Massachusetts, the chapter of the National Association of Social Workers (NASW) has recommended that social work students identify themselves as trainees, interns, or students either verbally or by using name tags and designate their status in the signing of any notes in official records.

Historically, many agencies haven't required students to identify themselves for several reasons: (1) students receive close supervision, (2) students typically have small caseloads allowing them to give more attention to each case, and (3) agencies did not want to create unnecessary problems for students or for themselves. Frequently agencies feel that students bring interest, enthusiasm, and commitment to their clients that results in a sense that clients get no worse service, and sometimes even better service, from student interns than they get from regular staff members.

In one agency that comes to mind, clients who cannot afford private counseling are told that they may receive help from a student immediately or wait six to ten weeks for a "free slot" to open up. Many clients choose students. However, clients who are not comfortable with students should be afforded other options.

Certainly, students should not be defensive or feel obligated to make self-deprecating remarks because they are students. Every professional has to start as a student. Hepworth and Larsen (1990) suggest that instead of saying "I will see you for eight sessions because that is all of the available time before school ends," one should say, "I will see you for eight sessions because that is sufficient time" (p. 599). The latter provides for a more positive working relationship and takes the emphasis off being a student.

Because we believe that clients should be informed about the qualifications of those providing services to them, we believe that generally students should identify themselves as such sometime during the first session unless the client is in crisis or makes a one-time or brief telephone contact.

How Do I Know if I Am Helping My Clients?

Two clients provide interesting illustrations for knowing when a client has been helped.

> The first client, a young woman, was brought to the community mental health clinic because of an inability to leave her home without fainting. The student soon discovered that the onset of the client's problem coincided with an incident when she had been brutalized by her former husband. He had kidnapped her from a parking lot and taken her to a remote spot, where he had tied her up and beaten her.
>
> The social work intervention consisted of empowering this woman by brainstorming and role playing the courses of action open to her in any situation in which she might again encounter her ex-husband. (She could carry a police whistle, carry a can of mace, drive with her car doors locked, etc.) After about six weeks, the client skipped her final session. A short time later it was learned that she was successfully employed in a department store. It was obvious that this client had been helped.

Another client had multiple problems and was resistant to solving them. She was obese and had low self-esteem. Her intelligence was slightly below normal. She had an alcoholic and unemployed husband and was herself unemployed and abusing drugs. The student displayed the same enthusiasm with this client as he had with the other client. He attempted to find her strengths and build on them.

> The client's happy moments seemed to be largely associated with a period of time when a local motel employed her as a motel maid. She enjoyed the camaraderie of working with the other women and having a paying job. She felt sure that the motel people would hire her back again. However, by the end of the semester, absolutely no progress had been made. She was no closer to going

back and asking for her old job than she had been the day she walked into the agency. She still had all sorts of domestic and personal problems. At the end of the summer, the student felt like a complete failure as he transferred the case to another social worker. This client obviously had not been helped at all.

The point of these two stories is that frequently there are clear, visible indicators that clients have improved (e.g., they quit drinking, secure employment, avoid getting into trouble with the law). Other times, it is practically impossible to detect any real growth or movement on the client's part. How is a student to evaluate the planned intervention?

Although the second of these two clients was more difficult and would have been a challenge for even an experienced social worker, the student would have had a greater probability of helping this client if clear objectives had been developed in the contract phase. Clients are often vague and have complaints such as, "I want to feel better about myself," or "I want to stop being so nervous." Sometimes they do not know exactly what is wrong except that they are feeling unhappy or blue. It is very hard to know when you have helped a client if the treatment goal is as ambiguous as to "help the client to feel better about self."

The key to knowing when you have helped a client is to identify a specific problem or behavior with which you can monitor improvement. If a client says, "I don't like myself," you need to ask, "How can I help?" or, "What are you doing when you begin thinking that you don't like yourself?" Such probing will usually lead to a specific behavior or situation that is troubling the client. For instance, the client who initially indicated that he did not like himself may be terribly shy and reluctant to begin dating. If the client would like himself better by becoming more confident to begin dating, then focus the intervention on this. The criterion for success can be the client's securing that first date. Or, if the client does not know anyone interested in dating him, the target behavior may be having the client approach four different persons within a 30-day period and asking for a date.

Another client who says that he does not like himself may actually be expressing a desire to lose weight. You need to clarify this. If in fact the client is seriously overweight and believes he will like himself better if he can lose 65 pounds (and this seems to be his major concern), then the target behavior becomes the loss of weight.

Behaviors that can be monitored and reduced include angry outbursts, physical punishment of children, tardiness or absences from work, or instances of saying yes when the client really wanted to say no. Because psychometric scales exist for measuring certain attitudes or attitudinal traits, scales can be administered at the beginning and toward the end of intervention to see if clients have made gains in self-esteem or assertiveness, or if they are less depressed or anxious. (A number of instruments for monitoring improvement in clients are contained in Corcoran & Fischer's *Measures for Clinical Practice,* 1994.)

The systematic monitoring of a client's progress is a research method known as single-subject or single-system design. It is beyond the scope of this book to explain these techniques in detail; however, you can refer to Royse (1995) or Royse & Thyer (1996) for more detailed instruction. However, the process essentially involves deciding on the target behavior to monitor, obtaining a baseline (an understanding of the frequency or stability of the behavior prior to intervention), beginning the intervention, and then recording or graphing any changes in the behavior. An illustration is presented in Figure 5.1.

Problem: Mrs. Smith's neighbors have reported her to child protection authorities because she frequently screams at her children. She is assigned to a social work intern for intervention.

Target Behavior: Parental screaming in the Smith household.

Baseline: A neighbor reported that Mrs. Smith screamed loudly at her young children at least on 20 separate occasions last week. Mrs. Smith does not deny that count. The baseline will be established at this point.*

Intervention: The dotted line after the 1st week indicates the beginning of intervention (see graph). Mrs. Smith is asked by the student intern assigned to her to keep a daily record of the number of times she loses patience and screams at her children. She is assessed as being quite motivated to learn more about parenting. Mrs. Smith readily agrees to attend classes on child care and to keep a tally of her verbal outbursts.

Explanatory Note: As you can see from the graph, Mrs. Smith has made steady progress in learning how to deal with the stress of being a parent and not exploding verbally at her children. It is quite clear from this graph that the student who had been working with Mrs. Smith was very successful in helping her to reduce the frequency of the target behavior.

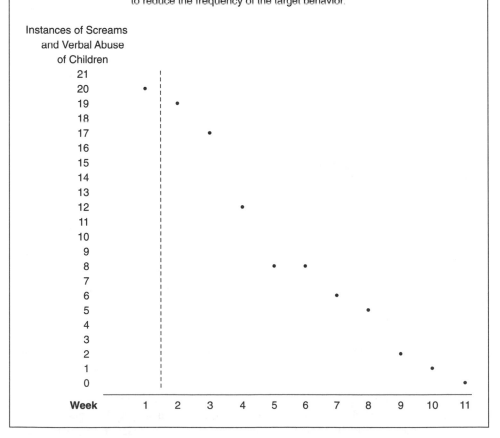

Figure 5.1   Single-subject design for intervention with Mrs. Smith

What Do I Do When a Client Won't Talk?

First of all, clients who have been ordered to receive services from an agency are not likely to be in a cooperative mood. They may have been threatened with going back to jail, with the loss of a job, or with the child protection agency taking custody of their children. Because of racism, poverty, and other societal factors, clients may resent your being a part of the system that has restricted or regulated their activities. Mandated clients may know about others who have committed the same offense and yet received a lighter sentence from the court. Okay, so they are angry. What can you do about it?

Give the contentious client an opportunity to tell you why he or she is so angry, but first go over the ground rules explaining about confidentiality and what your role is. Be willing to listen to the client's side of the story. (Ask "what" questions that allow a client to describe a course of events instead of "how" or "why" questions that ask for an explanation.) Ask the client what help he or she needs or what assistance you can supply; then explain the intervention or assessment procedures. If the client is sullen and will not talk with you, then give the client permission not to talk. Do not threaten or attempt to force a client to talk. If beverages are available, inviting the client to have a cup of coffee might help to reduce tension and the formality of the situation.

If the client still will not talk, explain that the client can sit there the whole 50 minutes without talking—not talking is a legitimate choice available to every client. However, you hope this will not be the client's decision. With a warm, accepting smile convey that you will be glad to talk during this scheduled time, which is after all the client's time. If the client chooses not to talk, then you can put the time to good use by completing paperwork at your desk. Finally, give clients the agenda for next week so that they can have ample time to think about what they want to discuss. Be patient. Some clients find it hard to trust and to make new relationships.

What Do I Do When the Client Who Won't Talk is a Child?

When clients are children, the unfamiliarity of office setting may frighten them. Reassure the child that the two of you just need to talk for a little while. If the child is particularly fearful, then acknowledge that children sometimes are a little scared at first, but that they soon forget that when they find how easy it is to talk to you. If after this explanation the child still will not answer any questions, do not show any frustration or anger—instead say, "That's okay. Let's do something different." Any agency that regularly has children for clients should have some toys available. Show the toys to the child and say, "I wonder what you'd like to play with?" Gabel, Oster, and Pfeffer (1988) suggest that at this point the child may involve you in the play and then begin talking. Sometimes you can encourage this by parallel play, or by making occasional remarks. If this does not work, they advise making something interesting from modeling clay or from paper and crayons. Ask for comments about what you are doing. Realize that with this type of child, the relationship will be built gradually, possibly requiring several sessions before the child feels comfortable enough to talk. If after your best efforts the child still will not communicate, try bringing in one or more family members to be with the child. Anxiety may be lessened when the child observes how other family members can converse with you without adverse results.

How Do I Manage Angry and Hostile Clients?

It is not uncommon for social workers to find themselves confronted with angry and potentially dangerous clients. Often these are involuntary clients who resent being forced into involvement with a social service agency. Unfortunately, you may become the object of resentment. Although their anger may not be directed to you as a person, you well may feel its heat and want to react defensively. Dealing with such clients requires a cool head and presence of mind in addition to familiarity with techniques that diffuse explosive situations.

First, try your best to stay calm and composed. Remind yourself that the client's anger may be natural and understandable given the situation. The client may have strong feelings of injustice. The system may have been too impersonal, bureaucratic, or inflexible. Because you represent the system to the client, he or she may be taking advantage of finding a sympathetic ear to unload anger and frustrations that have been building over time.

As much as possible, try to be empathic and understanding. Allow these clients to talk and explain why they are so angry. Speak in a soft voice and move slowly. Sheafor, Horejsl, and Horejsl (1994) recommend that you avoid touching an angry client or moving into his or her personal space. Sit if you can; standing is a more aggressive position. (However, do not position yourself in a corner or behind furniture, where it would be difficult to get out if escape becomes necessary.) Encourage the client to sit.

By not reflecting back the client's anger, you should be able to influence the client's behavior positively. More than likely, the client will be watching how you react, and so you need to be aware of how your actions can be interpreted. If the client is agitated, use the same techniques that you would use for a nervous client; for instance, ask if you can get the client a cup of coffee or something to drink. Trust your intuition. If you sense that you are in danger of being hurt, get out of that situation as quickly and coolly as possible. Say that you need a drink of water, or that you have to check on something—then leave the room and seek help.

Above all else, do not take risks that will jeopardize your personal safety. If your intuition tells you that a situation is dangerous, do not plow headstrong into it because you don't want to be embarrassed that you couldn't handle it. Always seek help when you sense that your safety or that of others is in danger. Discuss with your field instructor and other staff members your apprehensions and ways to handle difficult situations. Such conversations may allay your fears or give you suggestions for ensuring your safety.

How Do I Protect Myself?

Tully, Kropf, and Price (1993) found that approximately one in four of the practicum students in their survey experienced "some type of violence" at their placement; 24% of the field instructors had experienced a physical assault from a client. Although it is not pleasant to think about, an irate client may verbally abuse you, curse and shout, threaten you with harm, or even assault. Do not be so naive as to think because you want to help others, they will always be polite, compliant, and appreciative. They will not. Some clients have poor impulse control and lack anger management skills. Others will be impaired by alcohol or drug use. The best protection you can have is to anticipate what *might* or could happen in any situation where there is potential for violence—and plan accordingly.

For instance, if your agency doesn't have a "buddy system," where someone would accompany you when making a home visit to a potentially explosive situation or when traveling into high crime areas, then talk to your field instructor about developing a plan. Consider taking another person along whenever you expect to be involved in cases outside the office where there has been continuing domestic violence, involuntary removal of a child, or where workers have been previously threatened or assaulted. Be alert for vicious dogs that could be unchained or let loose. You may need to request a police officer to accompany you whenever entering potentially volatile or risky situations.

Routinely when traveling outside of the agency, keep someone informed of your destination, the length of time you expect to be there, and the time you expect to arrive back at the agency. If your appointment is at the end of the day or after dark, have an agreement with the person to whom you tell your destination that you will call when you have arrived safely back home.

Additionally, we suggest that you take a multipronged approach that considers all the major elements of an assaultive situation. Start with a plan—what you might and could do if trouble threatens. Consider taking self-defense classes along with the following:

1. Agency-related suggestions
    a. Learn the agency's established procedures for dealing with violent situations. If there are none, talk with your field instructor about developing procedures.
    b. Find out who you should contact when you need emergency help. Have important phone numbers (e.g., security, police) in a prominent place beside the phone.
    c. Take advantage of the informal communication system within the agency to learn of clients who are known to be violent and the best approach for handling them.
    d. Be aware of conditions in the agency, such as long waiting periods, that might be conducive to frustration and anger. Do what you can to improve these conditions.
2. Client-related suggestions
    a. Try to understand why the client is angry.
    b. Try to maximize the client's control over decisions that affect him or her.
    c. Try to reduce the client's feelings of insecurity and powerlessness.
    d. As part of your assessment, try to learn what has helped the client to manage frustrations and crises in the past.
3. Worker-related suggestions
    a. Avoid the "John Wayne" syndrome; do not try to meet force with force. Always show the client respect.
    b. Avoid finding fault, asking "how could you" questions, ridiculing, arguing, or coming across as uncaring, inattentive, or aggressive.
    c. Avoid such mistakes as excessive familiarity with clients—"potentially assaultive clients, may perceive casualness or gestures of familiarity as abdications of the professional role and. . . fear. . . that staff are not going to

protect clients from their own hostile impulses" (Murdach, 1993, p. 311).
Set and enforce limits when necessary. Don't give too much control to
clients who are incapable of providing their own structure and direction.
And don't rely too much on coercion and restriction to control client
behavior.

d. Be aware of your own typical responses to emergency situations; think
about how those responses might either encourage or discourage assaultive
behavior.

e. Learn the techniques that have been found to be helpful in such hostile situations. Neither passivity nor aggressiveness on the part of the worker is as
helpful as assertiveness. When a client or patient is becoming hostile, passivity can come across as fear or helplessness or as acceding to the threat.
Aggression can be interpreted as a challenge or a dare. Either suggests a
power struggle, but assertive communication can have a preventive effect.

f. Make sure the office furniture is arranged so that it is easy to escape if an
assaultive situation seems imminent; avoid having the client sit between
you and the door.

g. Be aware that jewelry such as large, dangling earrings and necklaces, and
other items of clothing (scarfs and ties) can be easily grabbed and used to
choke or pull you.

How Do I Deal with Noncompliant Clients?

Noncompliance is very frustrating, particularly when the client seems to be relating well
to you, owns up to the problem, agrees with the plan to do something about the problem,
but fails to keep appointments or does not complete expected tasks. Although the reasons for noncompliance are not always clear, these clients tend to be labeled "resistant"
and "unmotivated," and workers may give up on these clients too easily.

Richardson, Simons-Morton, and Annegers (1993) have used values expectancy
theory to suggest that when the costs of treatment outweigh the expected benefits, people chose noncompliance. The "costs" of compliance need to be viewed much more
broadly than expenditures of finances or time. For instance, there is the cost of changing
habits and altering lifestyle, the cost of acknowledging and dealing with a disease or
health risk, and the cost of submitting to outside authority and losing control of one's life.

You may find the following suggestions helpful in dealing with noncompliant clients:

- Try to understand what it will "cost" to change from the client's perspective.
Examine the disadvantages and obstacles to change as well as the benefits.
Being "sick" can be more gratifying than being well. What is lost when one
becomes "well"?

- Recognize that noncompliant behavior may be the client's way of dealing with
overwhelming circumstances, an attempt to reestablish personal dignity and
control, attention getting, or even a need to express rage or hurt.

- View noncompliant behavior as taking place within a context where motives
are competing or in conflict. The client may be experiencing problems but still

be stuck in denying their severity or their larger ramifications. Examine your problem-solving strategy. Does it ask too much of the client?

- Provide encouragement to clients, and reinforce the efforts they make toward compliance. Watson (1994) found that an inexpensive follow-up procedure, a second encouraging phone call, increased the compliance of clients who were initially noncompliant with referral recommendations of employee assistance counselors.

- Convey the expectation that clients assume responsibility and become compliant. You may have to help clients achieve an optimal balance between discomfort and hope. This can be done not only by encouraging clients to recognize the extent of their dissatisfaction with the problem and the hurt and anxiety it causes, but by also building on the hope that the problem *can* be solved with effort.

Clients can be noncompliant in many ways—one of the most common is for them to continue to drink or do drugs when they are supposed to be abstaining. Many agencies have policies that require clients to be sober in order to receive services. If you smell alcohol on a client's breath or have good reason to suspect that he or she is continuing to abuse drugs, then you may have no choice but to temporarily or permanently suspend services. But before you confront a client about this type of noncompliance, be clear about your agency's policies and how your supervisor would want you to inform the client.

Why Do I Need to Work with Clients Who Are Different from Me?

Demographic trends and other societal changes taking places in the country suggest that the U.S. population will continue to become more diverse racially, culturally and ethnically. Social work practitioners will increasingly be required to have knowledge about these populations, as well as the sensitivity and skills to work effectively with them. The new Curriculum Policy Statement of the CSWE requires all social work programs, both BSW and MSW, to cover *diversity, populations-at-risk* and *promotion of social and economic justice* along with *social work values and ethics* as part of the professional foundation content.

You can expect in a social service practicum to encounter many kinds of clients. They may differ in religious beliefs, skin color, age, sexual preference, lifestyle, native language or country of origin, socioeconomic class, and hundreds of ways that are not easily anticipated. You may discover physicians who are wife beaters, social workers who are alcoholics, and clergy who are adulterers. Many of your idealized images or stereotypes about people will undoubtedly be shattered as you learn that all humans have the same basic needs and foibles.

Case Example————————————————————————————

Walking to class one day, a social work student you barely know informs you that he could never work with gay or lesbian clients. He says that he would get rid of them as quickly as possible if he were ever assigned this type of client. You are too stunned to reply. You sense that this student is terribly homophobic. You wonder whether this student has ever read the NASW Code of Ethics.

Questions

1. Does the biased student have a good understanding of social work values?
2. What would you say to the student?
3. Would the situation be any different if the student had said that he could not work with African Americans?
4. What if he had said that he could not work with alcoholics or child molesters?

How Do I Work with Clients Who Are Different from Me?

Maslow (1970) has helped us to understand that in addition to food, water, oxygen, and safety, we all have needs to belong and love, to achieve and be competent, and to fulfill our unique potential. We need others to value or appreciate us and to think that we are important. These things are essential, no matter what our skin color, gender, or native language. We can always relate to other human beings when we think about the things that we have in common. Although we may differ on what constitutes the "good life," most of us want to be safe and secure, to have enough food, to have our loved ones around us, to have access to medical care and entertainment, and to have outlets for work or creative expression. *Recognize universal human needs.*

Sometimes, however, it is possible to "universalize" too much. Not everyone will like the same foods as you, nor agree with your notion of the best presidential candidate or the best religion, nor express his or her sexuality in the same way as you. We all have common human needs, but as human beings we sometimes seem driven to differentiate ourselves from others. Some of these differences are cultural, acquired in the process of living and growing up, learned unconsciously. Clients' unique needs are the result of the interplay of individual personality and cultural factors. *Do not over-universalize the commonality of human needs.*

To work effectively with clients, social workers must recognize, understand, and accommodate both their universal and unique needs. Ignorance of a client's culture has to be overcome consciously. Students can learn about the unique characteristics of others by reading, observing, listening, and being sensitive to the fact that not everyone will have the same preferences and values. *Realize that clients are simultaneously similar to others and unique.*

Until you understand them better, you may find that clients from different cultures or backgrounds are not as open with you as they may be with other staff. Because of language difficulty or other factors that make you feel uncomfortable around them, they may sense that you do not accept them. If a client from another culture is resistant, ask yourself if you are viewing the client in a stereotypical manner or judging narrowly from your own cultural perspective. If the answer is yes, then you will probably want to talk with more experienced staff members or your field instructor about techniques to try with this client. Do not rely blindly on standard counseling techniques with clients from other cultures without questioning whether these or other techniques are more appropriate. At a minimum, do some reading on how to work with this population. *Consciously avoid taking a stereotypical view of people.*

When working with people who have different values, it is probably inevitable that some clash will occur. Such incidents present opportunities for students to examine their own values. When working with clients remember that professional values take precedence over personal values. Social workers do not have the right to impose their religious or moral values on others. Ethical practice entails making the welfare of the client the primary obligation and providing service that is nondiscriminatory. Every client is entitled to fairness, equal access to services, respect, impartiality, confidentiality, empathy, and a nonjudgmental attitude. Students who allow biases and prejudices against other persons to interfere with the quality of care provided to clients violate professional ethics. Unless they are willing to do some intensive self-examination and make a mighty effort to accept diverse clients, these students should seriously consider another line of work. *Remember that the client's welfare is your foremost concern.*

Here is a list of practice intervention strategies found to be effective for assessing culturally diverse clients.

- Consider all clients as individuals first, as members of minority status next, and as members of a specific ethnic group last. This will prevent over-generalization.
- Never assume that a person's ethnic identity tells you anything about his or her cultural values and patterns of behavior. There can be vast within-culture differences.
- Treat all "facts" about cultural values and traits as hypotheses to be tested anew with each client.
- All minority groups in this society live in at least two cultures—their own and the majority culture. The difficulty of surviving in a bicultural environment may be more important than their cultural background.
- Not all aspects of a client's cultural history, values, and lifestyle are relevant to social work. Only the client can identify which aspects are important.
- Identify and build on the strengths in the client's cultural orientation.
- Be aware of your attitude about cultural pluralism.
- Engage the client in the process of learning what cultural content—beliefs, values, and experiences—is relevant for the work together.

These additional suggestions come from Dillard (1983):

- Be aware that the nonverbal component constitutes more of the communication than its verbal component.
- Recognize that eye contact can be a problem for many ethnic groups.
- Use self-disclosure judiciously.
- Summarize from time to time.
- Use confrontation carefully with certain racial groups.
- Remember that openness, authenticity, and genuineness are respected in all cultures.

What is it Like to Work with Small Groups of Clients?

Many agency supervisors give students opportunities to observe, participate in, and some-times, to lead groups. Groups may be categorized in several ways; perhaps the most com-mon scheme divides them into either task- or treatment-oriented groups (Kirst-Ashman & Hull, 1993).

Task groups exist to achieve specific goals and objectives. These goals determine how the group operates, which roles members play, and how the social worker functions with-in the group. Task groups include boards of directors, task forces, committees and com-missions, legislative bodies, social action groups, agency staff, and multidisciplinary teams. Treatment groups include growth, therapy, educational, socialization, and support groups.

Many times field instructors can help you begin to understand the various roles that social workers assume within groups, for example, educator, facilitator, evaluator, listener, negotiator, and energizer. They can also help you build on or develop skills in motivating, helping all group members participate, checking overly aggressive members, developing win–win outcomes, stimulating the discussion process, recognizing and resolving con-flict, encouraging team building, and structuring group meetings.

Many students enjoy working with groups because they can cultivate their leadership skills while helping others to develop new problem-solving strategies. At the same time, going into a group of individuals that you do not know can be scary. Unless you have been given the role of leader or facilitator, it is probably best that you not come on too strong in the first meeting or two with a group; rather, listen and observe the natural group processes.

Will I Be Working with Families?

Yes, often the family is the focus of social work services because problems faced by an individual are generally influenced by dynamics within that person's family.

A family group has many characteristics of a small group but is also distinct for at least three reasons. One is that it is intergenerational, extending over long periods of time and with strong emotional bonds. Second, a family is a well-established system in which each member plays an important role. Third, family problems belong to the whole family, not just to particular members (Johnson, 1995).

Social work students need to develop an understanding of the wide variety of forms that families take in our society. They must acquire skill in assessing a family and its situation and then creatively devise, with the family, strategies for solving its problems. Volumes have been written on effective family therapy, and it is well beyond the scope of this book to cover that. Students may, however, find that Zastrow's (1995) summary of the theoretical frameworks of Virginia Satir, Salvador Minuchin, Jay Haley, and Ivan Boszormenyi-Nagi a good place to start learning more about various strategies for working with families.

What is Macro Practice?

Community organization is another term often used synonymously with macro practice. Community organization refers to various methods of intervention where collections of individuals are helped to deal with common social problems. The major tasks include identifying problems, formulating plans, developing strategies, mobilizing resources, and implementing, monitoring, and evaluating the plans.

Macro practice can also include administration of social agencies, interagency coordination, fund-raising, political action, and public education campaigning. Even in an agency that primarily serves individuals and families, students can develop community organization skills. Most social service agencies are involved in macro practice in one fashion or another—most commonly these are interagency case conferences, community needs assessment and planning activities, and public education projects.

Advocacy for groups of clients with specific problems is still another form of macro practice. Advocacy is championing the rights of others through direct intervention or by empowering clients to represent themselves. The NASW Code of Ethics states that advocacy is a basic social work obligation—that ethical behavior requires us to eliminate discrimination, to ensure equal access to services and opportunities, and to bring about changes in policy or legislation that improve social conditions and promote social justice. However, social service agencies and institutions sometimes create limitations on the practice of advocacy within the organization because of political implications related to funding bodies and public support.

To be an effective practitioner at the macro level, you will need to know about the community in which your agency is located. You should have at least a beginning knowledge of the historical, economic, political, and religious structures in that community. Such information should help you to understand how decisions get made in the community and what factors influence them (Sheafor, Horejsi, & Horejsi, 1994). Ask your field instructor to structure opportunities for you to develop macro-level skills as well as micro-level ones.

Ideas for Enriching the Practicum Experience

1. Are there any one- or two-day workshops or seminars being offered nearby that would improve your social work skills? If so, ask your field instructor for permission to attend appropriate workshops. If there is a fee for these workshops and you cannot afford to attend, then contact the persons conducting the workshops to see if there are scholarships or if you can attend by working (e.g., helping with the registration table).

2. Visit the agency library and find out the major journals which they receive. Browse these for interesting articles that may help with the clients you have been assigned. If your agency does not have its own library, then ask your field instructor about the journals that he or she reads or recommends for you. Leaf through these.

3. Select one of your clients and draw up a single-subject design as discussed in this chapter. Are your intervention goals narrow enough that it is easy to specify a target behavior to be changed?

4. Ask if a program evaluation has been conducted recently for the program under which you are interning. Read the evaluation to see how successful the program is. What recommendations did the evaluators make? What recommendations would you make?

5. Determine if within your agency there is a staff person assigned to do community education. If possible, accompany this person to a public speaking engagement. If no one in the agency does substantial public speaking, then try to find out why not. In what way might the agency benefit from organizing a speaker's bureau?

References

Corcoran, K., & Fischer, J. (1994). *Measures for clinical practice: A sourcebook.* New York: Free Press.

Dillard, J.M. (1983). *Multicultural counseling.* Chicago: Nelson-Hall.

Feiner, H. A., & Couch, E. H. (1985). I've got a secret: The student in the agency. *Social Casework, 66*(5), 268–274.

Gabel, S., Oster, G., & Pfeffer, C. R. (1988). *Difficult moments in child psychotherapy.* New York: Plenum Medical.

Germain, C., & Gitterman, A. (1980). *The life model of social work practice.* New York: Columbia University Press.

Hepworth, D. H., & Larsen, J. A. (1990). *Direct social work practice.* Belmont, CA: Wadsworth.

Johnson, L. C. (1995). *Social work practice: A generalist approach.* Boston: Allyn & Bacon.

Kirst-Ashman, K. K., and Hull, G. H. (1993). *Understanding generalist practice.* Chicago: Nelson-Hall.

Maslow, A. (1970). *Motivation and personality.* New York: Harper & Row. (Originally published 1954.)

Miller, J. & Rodwell, M.K. (1997). Disclosure of student status in agencies: Do we still have a secret? *Families in Society, 78*(1), 72–83.

Murdach, A. D. (1993). Working with potentially assaultive clients. *Health and Social Work, 18*(4), 307–312.

Reamer, F. G. (1991). AIDS, social work, and the "duty to protect." *Social Work, 36*(1), 56–60.

Richardson, M. A., Simons-Morton, B., & Annegers, J. F. (1993). Effect of perceived barriers on compliance with antihypertensive medication. *Health Education Quarterly, 20,* 489–503.

Royse, D. (1995). Single system designs. In *Research methods for social workers.* Chicago: Nelson-Hall.

Royse, D. & Thyer, B. A. (1996). Single system research designs. In *Program evaluation: An introduction* (2nd ed.). Chicago: Nelson-Hall.

Sheafor, B. W., Horejsi, C. R., & Horejsi, G. A. (1994). *Techniques and guidelines for social work practice.* Boston: Allyn & Bacon.

Tully, C. T., Kropf, N. P., & Price, J. L. (1993). Is field a hard hat area? A study of violence in field placements. *Journal of Social Work Education, 29*(2), 191–199.

Watkins, S. A. (1989). Confidentiality and privileged communications: Legal dilemma for family therapists. *Social Work 34*(2), 133–136.

Watson, M. E. (1994). *Compliance with referral recommendations from an employee assistance program.* Columbia University Ph.D. Dissertation.

Zastrow, C. (1995). *The practice of social work.* Pacific Grove, CA: Brooks/Cole.

Additional Reading

Chau, K. L. (1990). Social work practice: Towards a cross-cultural practice model. *Journal of Applied Social Sciences, 14*(2), 249–275.

Corey, M. S., & Corey, G. (1989). Dealing with difficult clients. In *Becoming a helper.* Pacific Grove, CA: Brooks/Cole.

Dhooper, S. S. (1997). *Social work in health care in the 21st century*. Thousand Oaks, CA: Sage.

Dhooper, S. S. & Tran, T.V. (1987). Social work with Asian Americans. *Journal of Independent Social Work, 1*(4), 51–62.

Garland, D. R., & Escobar, D. (1988). Education for cross-cultural social work practice. *Journal of Social Work Education, 24*(3), 229–241.

Green, J. W. (1995). *Cultural awareness in human services: A Multiethnic Approach*. Needham Heights, MA: Allyn & Bacon.

Hardman, D. G. (1975). Not with my daughter, you don't! *Social Work, 20*(4), 278–285.

Jacobs, C., & Bowles, D. D. (1988). *Ethnicity and race: Critical concepts in social work*. Silver Spring, MD: National Association of Social Workers.

Proctor, E. K., & Davis, L. E. (1994). The challenge of racial difference: Skills for clinical practice. *Social Work, 39*, 314–323.

Scalera, N. R. (1995). The critical need for specialized health and safety measures for child welfare workers. *Child Welfare, 74*(2), 337–350.

Takaki, R. (1994). *A different mirror: A history of Multicultural America*. New York: Little, Brown & Co.

Chapter 6

The Student Intern: Needed Skills

Overview

This chapter is designed to help students feel less nervous about beginning to work with their clients by providing a brief refresher on topics usually covered in students' practice courses.

Do Most Student Interns Feel Nervous and Inadequate?

Yes, probably a majority of students beginning a new practicum can expect to experience some nervousness—which does not indicate that students are not suited for social work, only that they want to do well and are aware that they have much still to learn. Changes in routines and new experiences involve an element of risk, which is always a little scary. Consciously or unconsciously student interns may think, "What if I don't do well in this placement?" "What if my agency supervisor expects too much?" "What if I can't help my clients?" or "Should I have taken additional classes before registering for the practicum?" In a study we conducted (Rompf, Royse, & Dhooper, 1993), about four of every ten students going into a practicum expressed self-doubts or felt deficient in the skills needed to perform well in their agencies. Students going into their first practicum were more anxious than students who had previously been in a practicum.

Logistical concerns can also be a source of anxiety. Questions may surface such as, "What if traffic is terrible and I am late the first day?" or "Where will I go for lunch?" These concerns can usually be managed by thinking ahead. To plan for the length of time it takes to travel, students can, for instance, drive to the agency a time or two before the practicum starts. They can look for a parking lot near the agency, or call the agency supervisor beforehand and ask where to park. And students can always pack a lunch for the first day until they discover where others in the office eat.

You should realize that it is okay to feel anxious—it is a common experience—and that making specific plans often helps to reduce the anxiety. In a book we recommend for students, Corey and Corey (1989) share some of their initial experiences in starting out:

In one of my earlier internships I was placed in a college counseling center. I remember how petrified I was when one day a student came in and asked for an appointment, and my supervisor asked me to attend to this client. . . . Some of the thoughts that I remember running through my head as I was walking to my office with this client were, "I'm not ready for this. What am I going to do? What if he doesn't talk? What if I don't know how to help him? I wish I could get out of this!" (p. 11)

Such anxieties and concerns are normal and all right for students to experience, because as social workers they will often have to support clients when they make changes in their lives. It is good for students to recall their own feelings when encountering change and new situations.

What Skills Might I Be Expected to Develop?

The diversity of human problems and their manifestation at different levels—individual, group, neighborhood, community, institutional, and societal—create the breadth of social work as a profession. Accordingly, different methods, approaches, and strategies have been conceived so that intervention can be applied in various situations and contexts.

The basic problem-solving method taught in practice courses is applicable across all situations and provides the basis for deciding how to intervene. Similarly, there are skills common to all levels of human organization. These include listening, observing, relationship building, interviewing, assessing, contracting, mediating, advocating, planning, and evaluating.

We expect that most students entering a practicum for the first time will be practicing micro-level skills. Although some students may go into macro-level placements without ever developing the skills required for working with individual clients, we think that this is rare. Most students start by learning how to work with clients one-on-one. The balance of this chapter will focus on the skills and problems that may arise in such settings.

How Do I Start Interviewing with a Client?

According to Kadushin (1972), social workers spend more time interviewing than in any other activity. It is the most frequently employed social work skill. In view of its importance, it is natural for student interns to feel somewhat uneasy whenever they begin to think about the responsibility of interviewing that first client. So relax a bit if you feel uneasy—most students (and probably clients, too) face the first interview with some apprehension.

It may help to realize that the physical environment gives you some measure of control during the interview. Freedom from distraction, privacy, and open space between participants in a room with comfortable furniture and adequate ventilation and light will make it easier for the client and for you. Check the interviewing room ahead of time (if the room is different from your office) to ensure that the temperature setting is right and that there will be enough chairs (e.g., if a family is expected). Sit in the room; get accustomed to it. Think of the questions you will need to ask. If you do not feel at ease there (e.g., insufficient privacy), then try to arrange for another office before the client arrives.

In a quiet office it is easier to feel relaxed, and to listen thoughtfully and give the client your full attention. Consider the arrangement of the furniture and whether it is better to sit behind the desk or away from it. Sitting behind a desk emphasizes the authority of the social worker and lends more formality to the meeting. Sitting away from the desk may help to create rapport a little more quickly.

An interview can be conceptualized as a three-stage process: (1) the opening, or beginning, stage, (2) the middle, or working-together, stage, and (3) the ending or termination stage. Each has a different focus and different tasks to be accomplished. Let us look at each of these stages in more depth.

The beginning stage starts when the interviewer greets the client, does whatever will make the client comfortable, and defines the purpose of the interview. Think of interviewing as a purposeful conversation. There is a specific reason that you will be talking with the client. After introducing yourself, therefore, it is often a good idea to ensure that the client is clear on the purpose of the interview. Always give the client an opportunity to discuss any special needs. In the initial interview, the intent is generally to learn about the client, the problem, the efforts that have been made to solve the problem; to identify untapped resources that may exist; and to find out what the client's expectations are of the worker and the agency.

It is safe to assume that the client has questions about the helping process (e.g., how the helping will occur, how long it will take, what it will cost). Imagine yourself as a client in a strange agency seeking help for a comparable problem. What questions would come to your mind? Answering these questions, and pointing out that the agency exists for clients with this type of problem, will assist in breaking the ice. Asking for help from strangers is not always easy, and in this phase it is important to help clients feel that they are in the right place and have made the correct decision.

As both of you begin to feel more comfortable, encourage the client to verbalize his or her feelings about the problem situation. An age-old social work maxim, "Begin where the client is," suggests that you attempt to understand the problem from the client's perspective. Avoid going into the interview with a preconceived idea about what the client is like or is apt to say. Do not form opinions too early or become guilty of stereotyping the client and hearing only what you have decided he or she will be saying.

Even while introducing yourself and describing the agency's policies, programs, and resources, convey an interest and a willingness to understand the client's point of view. Each of your communications should reflect an interest in the client. For instance, gently probe, inquire, guide, and suggest. Do not cross-examine, make accusations or demands, or dominate. Both verbal and nonverbal messages should express an interest in the client.

The character of the case and the personal characteristics of the client will influence the interviewing process. With some types of problems, you will need to proceed more slowly than with others. The middle stage of the interview process is purpose-specific. You will be monitoring your communications for their effectiveness in keeping the interview on course, refocusing the client if the interview begins to drift away from its purpose, and possibly renegotiating a contract if that is indicated. When the purpose of the interview has been fulfilled, or just before the agreed time for ending the interview has been reached, the interview has reached the third stage.

During the termination stage, summarize what has happened during the interview. Agree on the next step (including the work to be done before the next interview and the purpose, time, and place of the next interview). Kadushin (1972) advises,

In moving toward the end there should be a dampening of feeling, a reduction in intensity of affect. Content that is apt to carry with it a great deal of feeling should not be introduced toward the end of the interview. The interviewees should be emotionally at ease when the interview is terminated. (p. 208)

Usually it is appropriate to engage in a few minutes of social conversation as a transition out of the interview.

Sheafor, Horejsi, and Horejsi (1988) suggest some helpful guidelines for interviewing:

1. Be prepared to respond in an understanding way to the client's fears, ambivalence, confusion, or anger during the first meeting.
2. Be aware of your own body language. The way you are dressed, your posture, facial expressions, and hand gestures all send messages to the client. Try to send a message of respect and caring.
3. If you have only limited time to spend with a client, explain this at the beginning of the session so the things of highest priority will receive attention.
4. Give serious attention to the presenting problem, as described by the client, but realize that many clients will test your competency and trustworthiness before revealing the whole story or the "real" problem. Begin with whatever the client considers important and wants to talk about.
5. Adapt your language and vocabulary to the client's capacity to understand.
6. If you do not understand what the client is saying, ask for further clarification or an example.
7. When you do not know the answer to a question asked by the client, explain so in a nonapologetic manner and offer to find the answer.
8. Explain the rules of confidentiality that apply to your meeting, and be certain to inform the client if what he or she says cannot be held in complete confidence.
9. If the client is bothered by your note-taking, explain why [notes] are needed, what will happen with [them], and offer to show the notes you have taken. If the client still objects, cease note-taking. If you are completing a form or following an outline, give the client a copy of the form to follow along with you.
10. Before the interview ends, be sure that the client has your name and the agency phone number, and that you have the client's full name, address, and phone number. (pp. 197–198)

To these we add a few of our own guidelines that will make it easier for clients to trust and feel that you are professional:

1. Never lie to a client or pretend that you have experience that you do not.
2. Do not make promises that you may not be able to keep or promises on behalf of others.
3. Do not argue with clients.
4. Do not attempt to force a client to tell you something that he or she does not want to tell. (If either you or the client are making frequent use of the word "but," then you are probably forcing some idea or line of questioning on the client. This will be experienced as more of an interrogation than an interview.)
5. Do not display (verbally or nonverbally) shock, surprise, or disbelief in response to what a client may tell you.

6. Do not talk down to a client or try to impress the client with your knowledge of clinical terms or jargon.
7. Although you may run out of time, do not rush the client. Realize that hesitation may be the result of anxieties or fears. Furthermore, do not finish sentences or supply words for clients in an effort to speed them up. If necessary, make a second appointment to complete the interview.

How Do I Begin to Help the Clients Who Are Assigned to Me?

Having acknowledged that you may feel a little insecure in your ability to help clients, let us quickly review what you should already know about the helping process:

1. The social worker makes use of self in helping clients. *Self* includes the knowledge acquired from the traditional academic environment, the common sense developed as a result of life experiences, and the social worker's personality. Social workers help clients to solve their problems through techniques such as listening, leading, reflecting, summarizing, confronting, interpreting, and informing. They support, explore alternatives, model behavior, teach, and sometimes refer. To help others, social workers should have self-awareness. They must know their own values, biases, strengths, and limitations. In reviewing the training of family therapists, Bagarozzi and Anderson (1989) discuss the sense of self as a primary vehicle for therapeutic change,

   > often evidenced in less of a tendency to "do things to and for clients" or to "give clients an intervention" and more of an emphasis on "being with clients" or "responding" to clients with greater genuineness, honesty, openness and courage. (p. 284)

   The necessary skills and knowledge to help clients are not easily specified—and probably reflect a constellation of abilities, knowledge, and experiences. Some social work students will be more aware of themselves than others; some will be more knowledgeable or more experienced. Many students can, however, make up for most real or presumed deficiencies in their expertise by being an active and interested participant in the helping process. Egan (1990) writes,

   > The best helpers are active in the helping sessions. They keep looking for ways to enter the worlds of their clients, to get them to become more active in the sessions, to get them to own more of it, to help them see the need for action—action in their heads and action outside their heads—in their everyday lives. (p. 105)

2. The first step in helping any client is establishing a therapeutic relationship. How exactly do social workers go about establishing such relationships? More than 30 years ago, Carl Rogers identified empathy, respect, and genuineness as being necessary for the therapeutic relationship. When these are communicated to clients along with a nonjudgmental attitude and an unconditional acceptance of their individual worth,

a relationship begins to develop. Without the social worker engaging the client or building rapport, the client is unlikely to share any personally important information. Patterson (1985) writes, "Counseling or psychotherapy is an interpersonal relationship. Note that I don't say that counseling or psychotherapy *involves* an interpersonal relationship—it *is* an interpersonal relationship" (p. 3).

3.   Once the social worker establishes rapport, he or she begins to explore and assess the client's problem. The social worker needs to understand what kind of assistance the client seeks, when the problem began, what factors complicate solving the problem, what efforts have been made, and what resources are available to the client. During this phase, the social worker finds a place to start the problem-solving process. Both client and social worker must agree on and choose some aspect of the problem causing trouble for the client. Often social workers support and encourage clients by providing them with hope that their present situation can be improved.

4.   When client and social worker reach agreement on what needs to be done and what realistically can be done, a contract is developed. The contract, which can be either written or verbal, provides focus and clarification—it serves as a reminder of what the client wants to achieve as well as what can be expected from the social worker.

5.   Implementation of the intervention or the actions covered in the agreement constitute the middle phase, or what Hepworth and Larsen (1990) call the "heart of the problem-solving process" (p. 33). They point out that "interventions should directly relate to the problems and to the consequent goals that were mutually negotiated with clients and that were derived from accurate assessment" (p. 33).

6.   When client and social worker achieve the contract goals, the final step in the problem-solving process follows. This step involves termination of the therapeutic relationship and evaluation of its results. Either the client or the social worker may begin a discussion about termination when some or all of the agreed goals have been achieved. Judgment about the appropriateness of termination is perhaps the easiest when the intervention is time-limited, based on a set number of sessions, or revolves around specific tasks (such as acquiring or extinguishing certain behaviors). Because many factors affect the decision to terminate, clients commonly drop out of therapy or express an interest in termination before achieving all of the stated goals. It is often appropriate to indicate that clients can return should they express an interest at some future time.

Should I Contract with Clients?

We believe that students are generally well advised to contract with their clients. Before we share some ideas about how to develop effective contracts with clients, however, we want briefly to discuss the concept of contract and its importance in social work practice.

The *Social Work Dictionary* (3rd edition) defines a *contract* as a "written, oral, or implied agreement between the client and the social worker as to the goals, methods, timetables, and mutual obligations to be fulfilled during the intervention process." A contract ensures accountability for all parties in performing the tasks essential for the agreed goals. Contracts are not always written; however, more and more social service agencies are moving in that direction.

The importance of a contract with a client follows from basic social work values, particularly the client's right to self-determination. Social work is not something done to clients; it is conducted with their cooperative efforts. Clients are expected to identify and rate the priority of their needs. Unless incapacitated, they are in the best position to determine what will be helpful to them (i.e., what courses of action to pursue) and when their needs have been met. Goals cannot be chosen for clients; they result from discussion, clarification, and other social work processes. During the course of intervention, a contract helps both social worker and client stay focused on the purpose of their work together. In addition to stating the agreed goals, the contract will specify the activities or interventions to be used, their frequency, any fees, and other agreements.

The essentials for developing contracts—discussed in Chapter 3—were derived from the SPIRO model (Pfeiffer & Jones, 1972)—which suggests (1) that *specific* goals be written, (2) that these goals be *performance* oriented, (3) that the *involvement* (roles) of the respective parties be stated, (4) that goals be *realistic* (feasible), (5) and that the results of your efforts be *observable* (measurable).

Contracting entails much more than we can tell you in this brief section. (If you need more information on the topic, you are encouraged to consult Hepworth & Larsen, 1990; Miller, 1990; or Sheafor, Horejsi, & Horejsi, 1997.)

What Do I Need to Know About Agency Recording?

Recording is an essential part of social work practice. The profession has always emphasized recording for two important reasons. First, it is assumed that there is an essential connection between good recording and the effectiveness of service. Second, recording is required in all types of practice in varied fields and settings. Its importance has been aptly explained by Siporin (1975): "The recording registers significant facts, evidence, judgments, and decisions about the people, problems and situations involved; it defines the reality of the helping situation and experience; presents the quantity and quality of service; and describes and explains the course of helping action" (p. 332).

Recording in social work may take many forms, from process recording—which involves a detailed narrative of all that happened during a client contact—to summary recording and the use of face sheets (intake or admission forms), agency documents, and reports of various kinds. Kagle (1984) has succinctly identified multiple ways that social service records can be used: to assess client and community needs; document services received and the continuity of care; communicate with others providing services to the client; supervise, consult, and educate students and workers; share information with the client; evaluate the process, quality, and impact of service; make administrative decisions; and do research.

Field instructors will orient their student interns to the recording requirements of their agency and will help students to learn how to fill out the various forms according to the breadth and depth of specificity required. Record-keeping can also be a valuable tool in students' own professional growth. Although it would be impossible to prepare students for every type of form that they will encounter on entering a practicum, we can share some general guidelines to help with agency recording.

First of all, keep in mind that the agency record is an official document. It is a permanent register that, while usually confidential, can be subpoenaed as legal evidence. This official record often includes highly personal anecdotes from clients' lives. Kagle (1984) observes, "The client's obligation to share personal information is predicated upon a reciprocal obligation on the part of the social worker and the organization—the obligation not to reveal this information except in specified, socially valued circumstances" (p. 116). This ethical duty is also a legal responsibility. Because of the sensitive nature of this material, confidentiality cannot be stressed enough.

Hepworth and Larsen (1990) provide several general guidelines for maximizing the confidentiality of agency records:

1. Record no more detail than is essential to the function of the agency.
2. Describe clients' problems in professional and general terms. Do not incorporate details of intimate matters except where necessary (e.g., a child's description of sexual abuse).
3. Do not include verbatim or process recordings in case files.
4. Do not remove case files from the agency except under extraordinary circumstances and then only with authorization.
5. Do not leave case files open on the desk or out in the open where they might be read by other clients or unauthorized personnel.

If you are in doubt about the level of detail to include, then discuss this matter with your field instructor. In some agencies, staff members may keep personal notes that are not a part of the official files. Your field instructor or faculty field liaison may even require you to keep a journal of your practicum experiences. Many agencies, however, discourage personal notebooks because of the risk that highly sensitive material could be misplaced, lost, or not safeguarded as well as agency files. Also, be advised that if you keep personal notes, these could be subpoenaed should your client be involved with or involve your agency in a legal suit. Therefore, if you want to keep a notebook, discuss this matter with your field instructor.

If you are permitted to keep personal notes, you may want to enter in them significant pieces of information about your clients and your impressions, analyses, or hunches. Since such notes could contain ideas or insights that are speculative and inappropriate for the official record, do not allow anyone else access to them, and do not keep them longer than absolutely necessary. Also, be sure not to use clients' full names, addresses, or other information that could personally identify them should you lose or misplace your personal notes.

There is much more to recording, and more specifically, to writing up a summary statement of an interview or assessment. *Summary records* are abstracts of a client's problem, the services provided to the client, and the client's progress. Agency policy specifies the form and content of such records. Because summary records may be subject to review by a number of people, it is usually good practice to include in them only that which is required and verifiable.

Many agencies rely on the problem-oriented record as a conceptual framework for cataloging essential information. Typically, staff members report both objective and subjective information as well as an assessment and treatment plan for the client. If your agency uses a problem-oriented approach, it is reasonable to expect that this process will be amply explained. However, if you need more explanation of this type of record-keeping, please refer to Appendix A. Because of its special educational value, we will discuss process recording separately.

What is Process Recording?

Process recording is a detailed narration of what happened during a social worker's contact with a client. Historically it has been used to monitor service delivery and assist in the development of practice theory. Field instructors and faculty field liaisons sometimes require student interns to do a process recording so they can examine the dynamics of the client-student interaction. It is an excellent teaching device for learning and refining interviewing and intervention skills. Process recording can help the student to conceptualize and clarify the purpose of the interview or intervention, to improve written expression, to identify strengths and weaknesses, and to improve self-awareness. Although they are often written exercises, process recordings can also involve audio or video taping, and live observation. (See Chapter 7 for more on audio and video taping.)

A process recording usually contains:

1. At least first names of those involved in the session
2. The date of the session
3. A description of what happened
4. The social worker's observations of the client's actions and nonverbal communications
5. The social worker's assessment of what happened and why
6. A diagnostic summary that pulls together the social worker's overall thoughts on the entire session (in a paragraph or so)
7. A brief statement of goals or plans for further contact with the client.

The actual description of what transpired can be written either with alternating lines for client and student intern, or as a narrative. When written as a script, the process recording can be used for role playing in supervisory conferences. For format, Wilson (1981) suggests the use of three or four columns. The first column is for the supervisor's comments and is left blank. The second column is used by the student to describe the content of the interview. The third column is used for recording the student's feelings as the dialogue takes place. Wilson believes it is difficult to put one's feelings into writing and that students may tend to use the third column to comment on the client's responses. If that happens, a fourth column should be added to analyze the client's responses. The use of these columns should help the student to develop diagnostic skills by providing a place for recording interpretations while forcing a separation of feelings from professional assessments. Other educators have suggested that the third column can be used simply for student reflection.

If you are required to do process recording, you will benefit from the following suggestions:

1. The time lag between the interview and writing up the process recording should be as short as possible. Since the process recording demands that you describe everything that takes place in the interview, you are likely to forget material with the passage of time.
2. Whenever possible, try to do process recording in conjunction with audio- or videotaping. This will help you to identify significant omissions and to remember things that you might otherwise have forgotten. (Remember to obtain both the client's and agency's permission and be sure that the taping will not unduly inhibit the client or negatively affect the session.)
3. Keep in mind that the purpose of process recording is to help you learn how to be a sensitive, effective practitioner. If you severely edit portions of the interview instead of allowing it to be verbatim, you may be depriving yourself of beneficial feedback.
4. Select the most challenging cases for process recording. Because process recording is a very time-consuming activity, it is likely that you will be required to do this type of recording on only a few cases. Choose a case that has the greatest potential for learning.
5. Take pains to ensure that your process recording does not jeopardize the client's confidentiality. Use a fictitious name for the client or perhaps only the first letter (Mr. C.). Keep the written records in a secure place. Remember that a process recording is a teaching device only. It should never become a part of the formal record of the agency.

You may want to follow this order in your process recording:

1. Purpose of the interview
2. Observations about the client's physical and emotional status
3. Description of the interview
4. Impressions (but based on facts)
5. Reflection on skills and techniques used
6. A plan for future contact and activity.

Although there are many ways in which to present a process recording, Figure 6.1 contains a streamlined example of one for you to visualize. This model does not separate out the student's feelings from his or her thoughts, although that can be a useful process, too.

I'm Self-Conscious About My Ability to Write Well. Will This Be a Problem?

Unfortunately, people who don't know us often form impressions about us on the basis of our written communications. Therefore, it is essential, if you want to be viewed as a competent professional, that your reports, memos, and progress notes show that you can communicate effectively and efficiently. This means your "formal" writing should be neat, free of misspellings and poor grammar, and should be punctuated correctly.

Look at the paragraph below to see what sense you get of the author:

The accused, I think his name was Bobie Meson or somethin like that was halucinating as he drove the Metro Bus into the city garage. He and his wife bough some LSD from a freind and they told Bobbie that, it would be safe to drive as long as he didn't take to much at one time. Carefully driving, the bus between parked cars until the Little Man with a gun. "Later." He ran and sat at a lunch counter and ordered a stake. That's were the police found them. The clinical staff recommended a 72-hour hold; and I agree: you can't be to carefull in this type of situation and need to seperate the details out from the lyes.

If you know yourself to be a poor speller, always consult a dictionary. Even better, type everything you can on a computer which has a spell-check function. Even this will not protect you from choosing the wrong homophone (like stake and steak) which the computer may recognize as correct although it could be an inappropriate choice for the passage you had intended. If the document is very important, have someone else proofread the final draft for you.

In terms of grammar, you may need to take a refresher course in writing skills. It is essential that you know when to capitalize and how to punctuate. If you are not sure of the rules, or if your papers typically come back from instructors with lots of red ink on them, this is a pretty good indication that you could use some help. If you are loathe to take another English course, at least make a trip to the library or bookstore and look in the reference section for writing guides. Consult these guides whenever you are in doubt about pronoun agreement, dangling participles, run-on sentences, sentence fragments, and the like.

Finally, take pride in your work by reading and revising. Proofread everything before you release it. Revise. If necessary, do two or three revisions. One of the best things you can do to improve your writing is to edit what you write. Remove unclear and unnecessary words. Polish. Don't be afraid to try and find another, crisper way of expressing yourself. Find someone in the agency who has a writing style you like, and then study it. Observe the points they make, and how they make them. Don't hesitate to ask for help. Your communication skills are important.

What Should I Keep in Mind When Making a Home Visit?

Social workers make home visits for many reasons. Whether student interns are observing, visiting a client with another staff person, or conducting their own home visit, they should be clear about the purpose of the visit. The purpose determines how the home visit is arranged, what content is covered during the interview, and what things are to be observed.

Many home visits are conducted to investigate possible cases of abuse or neglect. After a complaint is issued, social workers go out as quickly as possible. Because they want to see exactly what is happening in the home, in as natural a setting as possible, they may not call ahead. Ideally on an initial investigation, two social workers (or one social worker and a police officer if the situation seems volatile) would visit. When going into unknown situations, an inherent element of danger exists and two persons together provide greater safety (see Chapter 5 for a more detailed discussion of safety concerns).

Furthermore, two workers can gather more information than a single social worker. They can divide their effort so that, for example, one speaks to a parent while the other

Background: This is the first contact with a four-year old patient in hospital. The purpose of this session is to establish rapport.

COMMENTS AND FEELINGS

Student: Good morning, Melissa. How are you today?

Melissa: *No response*

Student: Did you have breakfast yet?

Melissa: *Nods her head affirmatively*

Trying to find a question she would have to answer.

Student: Let me guess what you had. Was it a big ol' baked potato? Was it a tiny little hot dog? Okay, then. . . was it one corn flake and a whole bowl of raisins. No? Then what was it?

Thought I'd try a humorous approach.

Melissa: Scrambled eggs and toast. (*smiles*)

Student: Did you gobble them all up?

Melissa: *Nods her head affirmatively*

More humor because she had smiled back to me.

Student: Good. Do you want anything else?

Thought I'd open things up to see what Melissa wanted to talk about.

Melissa: Where's my Mommie?

A break-through!

Student: Well, after the wreck they took her to another hospital. Do you remember the wreck last night?

Wanted to give Melissa opportunity to ventilate about the wreck.

Melissa: *Nods with downcast eyes*

Student: Wrecks can be pretty scary. Can't they? Do you want to talk about the wreck you were in?

Another opportunity for ventilation.

Melissa: *Shakes her head "no"*

Student: Okay. Maybe later, if you want. Say, I know. Want to go for a wheel-chair ride? This floor of the hospital has a whole bunch of kids and you know what? Some of them have IV fluids dripping into their arms just like you! We might even find anoth-er little girl with a broken leg. Want to see if we can find one?

Since she doesn't want to talk, thought she might be reassured by seeing other children. It also gives her occa-sion to raise questions about medical procedures or how other kids are getting along with their injuries.

I didn't want to give her more informa-tion about her mother than she needed. At least, not until Mom's con-dition stabilizes a bit more.

Melissa: Un-huh.

FIGURE 6.1   Example of a process recording

talks to the children. This arrangement allows for less manipulation by the client. Going into a different room or part of the house also allows greater opportunity to observe ventilation, heating, sanitation, and safety hazards within the home.

Clients on investigative home visits are often frightened and intimidated and will perceive you as an authority figure. Clients may be angry about the allegations made against them. Although you can be empathic about their feelings, you are required to explain your job clearly. Try not to be threatening, as you need to lay the groundwork for potential future social work intervention.

If the purpose of the home visit is to offer assistance, then it is almost always best to call ahead and ask clients when you may make a visit. This enables more efficient use of your time—you will be less likely to find no one at home. Giving notice also conveys an attitude of respect for the client's privacy and recognition that the client's time is important and should not be inconveniently interrupted. Many people do not enjoy it when others just show up on their doorstep—particularly people they do not know well. Another advantage of informing these clients ahead of time is that they can gather any necessary papers or documents.

As you enter a home, it is usually a good practice to engage in small talk for a few minutes until the client has a chance to relax a bit. You can thank the client for his or her directions, mention something you saw as you drove or walked to the client's house, or comment on objects you see in the home—photographs of family members, homemade articles, collections that might indicate hobbies, or books or magazines being read.

One of the main advantages of making a home visit is that you can gain a much better understanding of how an individual or a family functions on a daily basis. In a short amount of time you can observe interactions among family members, assess the family's resources, and begin to understand what a day in the life of your client is like.

Almost every student intern is nervous the first time that he or she makes a home visit. With experience, you will feel more and more at ease. One child protection worker recounted his first home visit as follows:

> I felt like a child playing a grown-up's game. How was I going to pull this one off? I remember being so nervous. I walked into the client's home, pulled out a notebook with a long list of questions, and in a very stiff manner began my interrogation. I scarcely lifted my head up to hear the answers. Now, several years later, when I run into my former client we always laugh about that first meeting. She, too, remembers being extremely nervous, so much so that she never realized how uncomfortable I was!

Plan on taking from 45 minutes to an hour for most home visits. If you know you will want to return, then ask when you can come back. Whether you take someone with you on a subsequent visit will depend on how the first visit went.

How Do I Refer a Client to Another Agency or Professional?

As professionals, social workers' commitment to clients demands that we make the best possible match between their needs and the resources most likely to help. A *referral* is the linking of a client with an agency, program, or individual professional who can provide a needed service. A referral to an outside resource may be made at the time of intake, at any time during the ongoing work with a client, or, often, while terminating service with a client.

Many reasons necessitate making a referral. You might identify, for instance, the need for a diagnostic service or consultation to assist with the intervention you will be providing to the client. On other occasions, the referral may demand a collaborative working relationship in which the referring agency coordinates services and retains primary responsibility for the case.

Here are some of the most common reasons for making a referral outside of an agency:

1. Lack of staff with necessary skills.
2. Lack of sufficient staff.
3. Clients have problems beyond the usual function of the agency.
4. Presumed superiority of the quality of some other agency's resources.
5. Presumed quantity of services available in another agency.
6. Another agency or program has been given responsibility for certain problems.

Referring clients to other resources requires careful work. Weissman (1976) has reported that within a group of individuals referred to an agency for service, 32 percent had no contact with the agency and another 20 percent had no involvement with the agency after the initial contact. Thus, in more than 50 percent of the cases, the purpose of the referral (linking a client with needed resources) had not been served.

The referral process involves several types of interventions and consists of three stages: advising and preparing clients for referral, referring and aiding clients in linkage with needed services, and following up on the referrals.

Generally, when you have identified a need that cannot be met at your agency, you should make a referral to an outside resource. Your first task in this stage is to advise the client of this and to make sure that the client agrees. The decision to seek additional help should emerge from your joint deliberation. It may be necessary for you to present information to help the client realize the necessity of the referral. Do not underestimate the resourcefulness of clients. Explore with them resources within their own natural support system (e.g., family, friends, neighbors) as well as other formal community agency resources.

While deciding together what resource would be the best match for the clients' needs, respect the clients' right to self-determination. Encourage clients to express their feelings about seeking additional help elsewhere as well as their feelings about the specific agency or professional being considered. Deal with any doubts, fears, or misconceptions about the resource being discussed. If brochures or pamphlets are available, share these and other information, but be careful not to make promises about what this agency or professional will do.

If the nature of the referral means that a client will have no further dealings with you, and if you sense that the client is feeling a sense of loss or ambivalence about terminating work with you, acknowledge that the time the two of you have spent together has been meaningful. Take pains to prevent the client from feeling that he or she is being rejected or betrayed. Do not sabotage the referral by giving covert messages that no one will be as caring as you are.

In the second stage of the referral process—referring and aiding clients in making the linkage—you will need to estimate the client's ability to make the necessary connections.

"Some clients can be given full rein to make a contact and complete the procedures on their own. Some clients need to be carefully rehearsed and escorted" (Siporin, 1975, p. 314).

When possible, use a multipronged approach. For instance, you may have the client schedule the necessary appointment from the phone in your office so that you can be there to assist. You may follow this by making a written request or report, getting the client's permission to share pertinent agency files, or helping the client to complete an application form.

Weissman (1976) suggests use of the following connection techniques:

1. Write out the necessary facts: the name and address of the resource, how to get an appointment, how to reach the resource, and what the client may expect upon arriving there.
2. Provide the client with the name of a specific contact person at the resource.
3. Provide the client with a brief written statement addressed to the resource describing in precise terms the nature of the problem and the services desired by the client. Involve the client in composing the statement.
4. In case the client is apprehensive or diffident about going to the resource alone, arrange for a family member or friend to accompany the client. You may choose to accompany him or her yourself. (p. 52)

The third stage of the referral process consists of following up with the client. There are several ways to go about this. You might ask the client to call you after the initial contact. Or, with the client's permission, you may call the client at a date after the scheduled first contact with the referred resource. Another approach is to plan a session with the client before and immediately after the scheduled appointment with the resource.

Your field instructor may need to assist you when making referrals that require a consultation or a collaborative arrangement. At times, your student status may work to a disadvantage because your authority is not equal to that of other professionals with higher status.

Case Example

An adolescent who has been having a difficult time with his parents is one of your clients. He is a bright 16-year-old who is attractive and personable. You like him a lot and suspect that he is more open with you than he was with his previous social worker. He is rather moody, however, and seems to be very depressed on occasion. Today, he seems more depressed than you have ever seen him. You suspect that he is planning either to run away from home or possibly to commit suicide. When you try to probe, he becomes uncooperative. You ask him to sign a contract agreeing not to commit suicide. He refuses, saying that it is unnecessary. At the end of the appointment, he gets up and says, "Maybe I'll see you next week."

Questions

1. Should you inform the adolescent's parents that he is potentially suicidal?
2. Should you arrange an inpatient hospitalization?
3. Is it necessary to involve your agency supervisor?

How Do I Know if a Client is Suicidal?

Every year there are slightly over 31,000 deaths attributed to suicide, but this figure reflects only known, successful suicides. Kaplan and Sadock (1988) estimate that the number of attempted suicides is eight to ten times larger. After accidents and homicides, suicides are the leading cause of death in the 15- to 24-year-old age group (Wodarski & Harris, 1987). Each year, about a half-million young people between the ages of 15 and 24 will attempt suicide. Predictors of suicide tend to include:

- mental disorder (substance abuse, affective disorders, schizophrenia, panic disorders)
- Age: persons 45 years of age or older are greater risks
- Gender (About four times more men kill themselves than women)
- Marital status: Divorced, separated, widowed, and persons never married are more likely to commit suicide
- Recent losses (resources, employment, relationships, status)
- Chronic physical illness
- Hospital discharge and apparent improvement
- Race: Native Americans and white men have higher suicide rates
- Previous attempts

Of these risk factors, clients with depression who express hopelessness, worthlessness, helplessness, or excessive guilt warrant special attention. Patterson et al. (1983) have developed a useful acronym to assist with evaluating suicidal patients. Their acronym is **S-A-D-P-E-R-S-O-N-S** which refers to: **S**ex, **A**ge, **D**epression, **P**revious attempt, **E**thanol (alcohol) abuse, **R**ational thinking loss, **S**ocial Supports lacking, **O**rganized plan, **N**o spouse, and **S**ickness. The risk for suicide can be assessed on a 1 to 10 point scale by assigning one point for each risk factor associated with the client. Hospitalization is recommended for patients scoring higher than 7. Strong consideration of hospitalization should be given to those who score 5 or 6, and a close follow-up is recommended for patients who score from 3 to 4.

Wollersheim (1974) has suggested using the following question to evaluate the patient: "You certainly seem to feel extremely depressed. Feeling this miserable, have you found yourself thinking of suicide?" There does not seem to be any evidence that talking directly about suicide will put ideas into the client's head. Instead, most clients would probably be relieved to have the opportunity to talk about suicidal thoughts (Sommers-Flanagan & Sommers-Flanagan, 1995).

Although it may not be unusual for most people to have at least considered the notion of suicide at some time in their lives, healthy individuals do not dwell on these thoughts. You should be concerned and mention to your supervisor any time that a client mentions suicidal ideation. Sometimes these are brief, passing thoughts; at other times they are recurrent and seriously considered notions. You should be especially concerned with any client who *frequently* has suicidal ideation, whose self-destructive thoughts are *intense,* or have significant *duration*.

Miller (1985) has recommended evaluating suicidal plans by assessing the four areas of: specificity of plan, lethality of method, availability of proposed method, and proximity of social or helping resources. These dimensions compose the acronym **S-L-A-P**. The more specific the plan, the greater the lethality of the method, the quickness with which the patient could implement the plan, and the further a patient is from helping resources, the greater the inferred risk of suicide.

What Do I Do if I Suspect My Client Plans to Attempt Suicide?

Once you have learned of suicidal intent or that your client scores high on a profile like S-A-D-P-E-R-S-O-N-S, your next step will be to ask the client directly if he or she is seriously considering suicide. Look the client in the eye and do not be shy or hesitant—this is a serious matter. If you have a good rapport with the client, generally he or she will be candid. If the client answers in the affirmative, then ask the client to contract with you not to attempt suicide without giving you time to help. Try to understand the depth of the client's despair. Do not minimize it. At the same time, try to infuse hope. Discuss the progress that the client has made. Point out the client's strengths and positive characteristics. Be optimistic and enthusiastic about what the two of you have accomplished.

If the client admits to planning suicide, or even if the client denies it but you judge the risk of suicide to be severe, you will need to discuss immediate psychiatric hospitalization. If the client does not agree to the hospitalization, inform him or her that in a situation such as this the policy is to inform your agency supervisor, responsible people in the client's life, and possibly the police. Immediately involve your agency supervisor, if possible, while the client is still in your office. You and your supervisor together may then decide to contact a family member, friend, or some other significant person in the client's life. In an emergency such as a suicide attempt, do not worry about breaking client confidentiality. "The duty to save a human life would take precedence over the duty to keep information shared by a client confidential" (Reamer, 1982, p. 584). Depending on the seriousness of the threat, protective actions (e.g., inpatient hospitalization) or involvement of legal authorities may be required even if the client objects.

Additional measures can be taken to manage the suicidal crisis. For instance, the client can be informed of your availability to be reached by phone. This can be accomplished between agency visits by making telephone "appointments" when the client may call you in your office and talk for a brief period. Inform the client of the availability of emergency psychiatric services and crisis counseling hotlines when you cannot be reached in your office. Although practitioners will sometimes give out their home phone numbers in situations such as this, students generally are advised against this practice. If it is vital that the client reach you at home, then leave your number with the community's 24-hour crisis hotline or the agency's staff so that you can return the client's call.

Remember that any time you are dealing with a suicidal client or even a client you suspect may be suicidal, you must inform your field instructor.

Case Example

In a new practicum you will be the case manager for five severely mentally ill persons. After a week of orientation and shadowing your agency supervisor, she hands you the files and asks that you contact the clients as soon as possible. With the first case, a 64-year-old woman with a record of seven hospitalizations over the past five years, there has been no contact for three months.

You try to reach the client by phone, and although it is a working number, no one answers. No one answers when you call again later in the morning and several times in the afternoon. The next day you make about six efforts to reach the client, but to no avail. There is no family member or close relative. You decide to make a home visit.

The client lives in a neighborhood where about every third house appears to have a junked and abandoned car in the yard. Wind-blown litter and trash is everywhere. The house where your client lives looks as if it should be condemned. The front porch is sagging badly and several of the floor boards are rotten. You knock on the front door, and for a moment you think you hear some movement inside. No one answers the door. You knock again louder, but with the same result.

Questions

1. Should you try to peek into one of the windows to see if you can see anyone or just terminate the case?
2. Should you go to the neighbors and ask them what they know about your client?
3. Should you call the police and ask them to assist you?

How Do I Transfer a Case?

Despite your best efforts, sometimes clients will not improve. In fact, they may get worse. This might have happened whether you were assigned to them or not. In other words, it may have nothing at all to do with you: it could be part of a cyclical illness like bipolar disorder, or result from poor decisions the client has made or environmental influences that you can't counteract. At other times, you may discover that there is something about a particular client that you dislike which makes it difficult for you to work with that person. If a client reminds you of someone like an abusive father, and you do not feel that you can be unbiased or provide the client with the same level of care you provide to others, then this is an argument for transferring the case.

Should you discover after a reasonable attempt and period of time that any client is not improving, you should at least discuss with your field instructor the possibility of transferring this case to someone else.

The staff person who is receiving the case may want to meet with you in order to go over the client's file and ask questions. Other staff may want you to arrange a meeting where you introduce the client and the new therapist.

The protocol for these meetings is for you to make the introductions, and to review the client's presenting problem, the strategies or steps the two of you have taken to address the problem, and what remains yet to be accomplished. If possible, point out any success or gains the client has made, and examples of changes the client has made—even if they are minor. Then, your role is to fade quietly into the background as the new therapist takes an active role and begins to raise questions of the client and to direct the remainder of the session. Do not answer questions for the client or take an active role after you have finished your summary.

Case Example

In transferring a client who had made little progress, Perry noticed that although he had used a cognitive approach with Sheila, the new therapist was primarily Gestalt-oriented. When the new therapist asked the client to describe her feelings about living with an alcoholic husband, Sheila looked at Perry with eyes that pleaded, "What's going on here? What have you done to me?" When he saw the tears in Sheila's eyes, Perry blurted out, "We've talked about this before, and Sheila doesn't want to leave her husband." Margot, Sheila's new therapist, glared at Perry and said, "Can I have a word with you out in the hall?"

Questions
1. Did Perry do anything wrong?
2. What should Perry have done?
3. Why would Margot try a theoretical approach so different from the one used by Perry?

How Do I Terminate Services with a Client?

Termination means the ending, limiting, or concluding of services. Not much has been written about termination in the helping process in social work literature. Possibly, this is because termination is an aspect of professional practice that resists precise definition.

Part of the problem in discussing the termination of services with a client comes from not knowing when a client will stop requesting services. Clients may decide not to appear for a scheduled second appointment or the planned final session. Premature and unilateral terminations by clients (i.e., terminations against professional advice) are often thought to represent unresolved resistance. Sensitive areas may have been opened up that the client is uncomfortable handling. This discomfort may result in strong denial or minimization of the problem.

Although students may be personally disappointed or feel that they have failed whenever they experience a premature termination, there are many reasons that clients may prematurely terminate services: the original problem may have actually improved in a short span of time; the client may have moved or be planning to move to another geographic area; there may have been major changes in the client's life (e.g., divorce from an abusing spouse or a prison term for that person). Other changes such as taking a new job, the birth of a child, or a serious illness of a close relative can make it difficult for clients to continue with a social service agency. If a student believes that a client needs further help, then the student may gently challenge the client's reasoning behind the decision to terminate, but ultimately he or she must respect the client's wishes. In such instances, it is advised that students inform clients that they can return to the agency if the need arises at some future time.

Termination of services also occurs when social worker and client jointly agree to conclude the service agreement. This may come about whenever either party believes that the client should be referred to another agency (e.g., for detoxification) or to another professional (e.g., a therapist who specializes in working with incest survivors). Termination may also be scheduled because both client and social worker believe that the original goals have been met, because progress is not being made, or because the practitioner is departing (e.g., the semester is ending for the student intern). In addition to premature termination, Hepworth and Larsen (1990) identify four other types of termination:

1. Planned terminations determined by temporal constraints
2. Planned terminations with time-limited modalities
3. Planned terminations involving open-ended modalities
4. Terminations due to the departure of a practitioner (p. 597)

Schools, hospitals, youth camps, and similar institutions are examples of settings where temporal factors determine when termination will take place. In these settings, there is a reduced chance that clients will interpret the termination as being arbitrarily imposed and have feelings of desertion or abandonment. The predetermined ending time, however, may not be appropriate for every client, and in such cases students must deal with the feelings (the client's as well as their own) that result from untimely separation. Where necessary, students will make arrangements for their clients to receive additional services.

Planned terminations associated with time-limited modalities involve the client's knowing from the beginning how long the service will last. This reduces the degree of emotional attachment and dependency, and the feeling of loss that clients may experience as the result of termination. Nevertheless, even in time-limited modalities, clients do form attachments and experience some sense of loss. Student interns must be sensitive to these reactions and allow the client to express these feelings.

In agencies where open-ended modalities of service are used, students need to begin thinking about termination when they start to feel that the gains from continued service will be minor at best. If the client has experienced improvement, but now progress has slowed considerably, then the student and the client should discuss this. If both concur that little recent progress has been made, then the client's options are (1) to take a furlough from services, (2) to cease services altogether, or (3) to continue with another practitioner.

It is not uncommon for students to feel a little nervous when thinking about termination—especially when a strong working relationship has developed. If the student suggests that his or her assistance is no longer needed, will the client feel rejection? Could the client regress? Students sometimes fear great damage might occur to the client if the termination is handled badly, but that thinking probably is not realistic. According to Epstein (1980), "It is a rare client who truly becomes unhappy or adrift when termination occurs" (p. 257). Nevertheless, the ending phase of the helping process is the culmination of all of the energies and efforts previously applied and should be taken seriously. Termination can be conceptualized as a series of discrete tasks, which you can review to help plan for the concluding of services with a client:

1. Determine the most appropriate time to conclude services.
2. Anticipate the emotional reactions commonly experienced.

3. Recognize the conflict in being helped and needing to move away from it.
4. Discuss what the client has learned, his or her strengths, positive changes in the client's thinking or life since beginning therapy. Point out how the problem-solving experience can be transferred to future problems.
5. Plan for the stabilization of the client's gains and continued growth.
6. Evaluate the service provided and the achievement of goals.
7. Emphasize the agency's continued interest in the client's well-being and suggest that he or she seek help again if needed.

The dynamics of each case will influence the way you actually approach termination with a client. Create in your mind a continuum for each of the concepts of emotional involvement, anxiety over termination, extent of problem resolution, and prognosis for future success. Different points on these continuums will characterize every client, and these positions will affect the way the client experiences termination.

Many authors have provided guidelines for effective termination. After reading this section, you may wish to consult several of the references at the end of the chapter for additional help with your termination efforts. But first we want to add a few guidelines from Egan (1990):

1. Plan for a termination in the helping process right from the beginning. (This can be accomplished in the client's service agreement or contract by setting an approximate ending date or the expected number of sessions.)
2. Be sensitive to any excessive dependency on the relationship which you or the client may have developed. Look for clues which suggest that the relationship has become more important than the problem management process.
3. State in the contract the degree of progress or change that would be sufficient for termination. End the helping process when it is clear that the goals have been accomplished.

Finally, with some clients who have become overly dependent, it is a good idea to take a gradual approach to termination by lengthening the time between sessions. During this process, make sure that the client is connected with other natural helpers, informal resources, or sources of social support. For clients who are terminating even though significant problems remain, you can suggest follow-up or booster sessions after official termination. Do everything to make a termination as positive an experience for the client as possible and to keep it from being abrupt or unexpected.

Ideas for Enriching the Practicum Experience

1. Discuss with your field instructor whether a good learning activity for you would be to attend a support group meeting outside the agency (e.g., Alcoholics Anonymous, Al-Anon). If you do attend, note what preconceived notions are broken as a result.
2. Find out if there are any films, videos, or audiocassettes that the agency has used in the past three years to train staff. Ask your field instructor if you may view or listen to these when you have no assigned or scheduled activities (e.g., a client cancels an appointment).

3. If your field instructor or faculty field liaison does not require a process recording or any recording (video or audio) of one of your sessions with a client, then ask if you may do one. Then, as part of supervision, ask your agency supervisor for feedback to make you a more skilled social worker.

4. What is the source of the majority of referrals to your program? What is the profile of the "typical" client? If no such information is available, ask your field instructor if you may spend some unscheduled time answering these questions from a random sample of 25 closed cases.

5. Browse through a recent issue of *Research on Social Work* or *Social Work*. Look for informative articles on issues, programs, or problems such as those that you commonly encounter in your practicum. Read relevant articles for your professional growth and share them with your field instructor and classmates.

References

Bagarozzi, D. A., & Anderson, S. A. (1989). *Personal, marital, and family myths: Theoretical formulations and clinical strategies.* New York: W. W. Norton.

Corey, M. S., & Corey, G. (1989). *Becoming a helper.* Pacific Grove, CA: Brooks/Cole.

Egan, G. (1990). *The skilled helper: A systematic approach to effective helping.* Pacific Grove, CA: Brooks/Cole.

Epstein, L. (1980). *Helping people: The task-centered approach.* St. Louis: Mosby.

Hepworth, D. H., & Larsen, J. A. (1990). *Direct social work practice: Theory and skills.* Belmont, CA: Wadsworth.

Kadushin, A. (1972). *The social work interview.* New York: Columbia University Press.

Kagle, J. D. (1984). *Social work records.* Homewood, IL: Dorsey.

Kaplan, H. I., & Sadock, B. J. (1988). *Synopsis of psychiatry.* Baltimore: Williams & Wilkins.

Keller & L. G. Ritt (Eds.), *Innovations in clinical practice: A source book* (Vol. 1). Sarasota, FL: Professional Resource Exchange.

Miller, L. J. (1990). The formal treatment contract in the inpatient management of borderline personality disorder. *Hospital and Community Psychiatry, 41*(9), 1009–1012.

Miller, M. (1985). *Information Center: Training workshop manual.* San Diego: Information Center, (As cited in Sommers-Flanagan and Sommers-Flanagan, (1995).

Patterson, C. H. (1985). *The therapeutic relationship: Foundations for an eclectic psychotherapy.* Pacific Grove, CA: Brooks/Cole.

Patterson, W. M., Dohn, H. H., Bird, J., & Patterson, G. A. (1983). Evaluation of suicidal patients: The SAD PERSONS scale. *Psychosomatics, 24,* 343–349.

Pfeiffer, J. W., & Jones, J. E. (1972). Criteria of effective goal-setting: The SPIRO model. In *The 1972 annual handbook for group facilitators.* La Jolla, CA: University Associates.

Reamer, F. G. (1982). Conflicts of professional duty in social work. *Social Casework, 63*(10), 579–585.

Rompf, E., Royse, D., & Dhooper, S. S. (1993). Anxiety preceding agency placement: What students worry about. *Journal of Teaching in Social Work, 7*(2), 81–95.

Sheafor, B. W., Horejsi, C. R., & Horejsi, G. A. (1997). *Techniques and guidelines for social work practice.* Boston: Allyn & Bacon.

Siporin, M. (1975). *Introduction to social work practice.* New York: Macmillan.

Sommers-Flanagan, J. & Sommers-Flanagan, R. (1995). Intake interviewing with suicidal patients: A systematic approach. *Professional Psychology, 26*(1), 41–47.

Weissman, A. (1976). Industrial social services: Linkage technology. *Social Casework, 57*(January), 5–57.

Wilson, S. (1981). *Field instruction: Techniques for supervisors.* New York: Free Press.

Wodarski, J. S., & Harris, P. (1987). Adolescent suicide: A review of influences and the means for prevention. *Social Work, 32*(6), 477–483.

Wollersheim, J. P. (1974). The assessment of suicide potential via interview methods. *Psychotherapy, 11*, 222–225.

Additional Readings

Baldwin, M., & Satir, V. (Eds.). (1987). *The use of self in therapy.* New York: Haworth Press.

Compton, B. R., & Galaway, B. (1989). *Social work processes.* Belmont, CA: Wadsworth.

Cormier, W. H., & Cormier, L. S. (1985). *Interviewing strategies for helpers.* Pacific Grove, CA: Brooks/Cole.

Fortune, A., Pearlingi, B., & Rochelle, C. D. (1992). Reactions to termination of individual treatment. *Social Work, 37*(2), 171–178.

Gutheil, I. A. (1993). Rituals and termination procedures. *Smith College Studies in Social Work,* 63(2), 163–176.

Jackson, H., Hess, P. M., & van Dalen, A. (1995). Preadolescent suicide: How to ask and how to respond. *Families in Society, 1995,* 267–280.

Kagle, J. D. (1993). Record-Keeping: Directions for the 1990's. *Social Work, 38*(2), 190–196.

Lurie, A., Pinsky, S., Rock, B., & Tuzman, L. (1989). The training and supervision of social work students for effective advocacy practice: A macro system perspective. *The Clinical Supervisor,* 7(2/3), 149–158.

Neuman, K. M. & Friedman, B. D. Process recordings: Fine-tuning an old instrument. *Journal of Social Work Education, 33*(2), 237–243.

Okun, B. F. (1987). *Effective helping: Interviewing and counseling techniques.* Pacific Grove, CA. Brooks/Cole.

Quintana, S. M. (1993). Toward an expanded and updated conceptualization of termination: Implications for short-term, individual psychotherapy. *Professional Psychology: Research and Practice, 21*, 379–384.

Siebold, C. (1992). Forced termination: Reconsidering theory and technique. *Smith College Studies in Social Work, 63,* 323–341.

Specht, H., & Specht, R. (1986). Social work assessment: Route to clienthood. *Social Casework, 67*(10), 587–593.

Weber, T. (1985). A beginner's guide to the problem-oriented first family interview. *Family Process, 24*(3), 357–364.

Woods, M. E., & Hollis, F. (1990). *Casework: A psychosocial therapy.* New York: McGraw-Hill.

Chapter **7**

Pragmatic Concerns

Overview

This chapter contains practical advice regarding situations and topics not covered elsewhere in the book. It provides answers to several miscellaneous questions that may arise during the social work practicum.

What Do I Do if I Get Sick or Am Running Late and Miss My Appointments?

It is probably inevitable that at some time during a practicum you will become ill, have car trouble, or experience another problem that may cause you to miss scheduled appointments. Once you know that you will be delayed or will miss an appointment, the professional course of action is to call the agency. Ask the secretary to contact your clients, your agency supervisor, and other involved parties to inform them of your absence. If you have an infectious illness (e.g., the flu), then it is much kinder to miss an appointment or two than to infect co-workers and clients. Appointments can be rescheduled when you are feeling better. If you are too ill to go to work, do not feel obligated to contact clients from home and provide routine counseling over the phone. If your car breaks down, and there is no phone close by, all you can do is to call the agency at the first opportunity. Once you are back in the agency, reschedule all missed appointments as soon as possible.

Case Example

Your car is undependable, and it is particularly difficult to start in the morning after it has been idle for eight or ten hours. You have taken the car to many repair shops, but no one can find the problem. You cannot afford to buy a new car now, and public transportation is not available within a reasonable walking distance of you.

Since beginning your practicum, problems with starting your car have made you late on three occasions. Once you were only 20 minutes late. The second time you were about 45 minutes late. On the third occasion, your agency supervisor sternly advised you to find another means of transportation because she had to see your client for you. After four frustrating weeks, you have just learned that your supervisor lives just a little over a mile from your apartment.

Questions
1. Should you ask if you can car pool with your agency supervisor?
2. What other options are available to you?

Will I Be Asked to Share a Desk or Office?

Student interns do not always have their own private offices. Often, they must share space with another student or students. Ideally, however, students should have their own desks and phones. When an office is shared with others (and it may be the field instructor), you should show consideration for others.

If you use a desk that is shared with another student or staff person, keep it tidy. Ensure that the working surface of the desk is clean before you leave each day. If you share an office, try not to monopolize it or the phone with loud conversation when your office-mate is working. Do not transform the office into your personal habitat. It is probably best if you do not bring in radios, televisions, or expensive personal effects to entertain you or to decorate the office.

If you share an office and you need private space for counseling, then the agency should have a vacant office for either you or your office-mate to use. Sometimes this space must be scheduled in advance. Be sure to learn the procedures for this before you find yourself with a client and no space suitable for interviewing. If the agency is critically short of space and on more than one occasion you and a client have to use an unsuitable area (such as a vacant corner of the waiting room), then report this to your faculty field liaison. The agency may not be well suited for the training of students. It is especially critical that the space or rooms utilized for working with clients not jeopardize their confidentiality by others overhearing or observing emotional responses.

How Do I Keep Track of Time in the Practicum?

You can keep track of the amount of time spent in your practicum placement by one of several methods. It may be simple enough to remember that you spend all day on Tuesdays and Thursdays and half of each Friday—for a total of 20 hours each week. Such a crude accounting system does not provide any description of *how* you spent your time. If asked about your major activities last week, could you recall them without the aid of some notes? It is important to keep a record of the hours you spend in an agency as well as the variety of experiences to which you are exposed. Reviewing this record from time to time can help you and your agency supervisor to monitor your progress toward your learning objectives and your development as a social worker.

Date _____

Student's Name _____ Agency _____

Hours Interned this Week _____ Cumulative Hours _____

Hour	Monday	Wednesday	Friday
8:00 8:30	Team meeting	Supervision with Field Instructor	Agency Research Project (Cont.)
9:00 9:30	Counseling Mrs. J	Staff Inservice	Preparation for Case Presentation
10:00 10:30	Writing Progress Notes and Treatment Plan		Counseling Mr. M
11:00 11:30	Preparation for Afternoon Group		Interview Children's Services Coordinator
12:00 12:30	Lunch	Lunch	Lunch
1:00 1:30	Observation Marital Therapy	Intake Desk	Staffing Crisis Phone Line
2:00 2:30	Counseling Jim C.	Intake Desk	Staffing Crisis Phone Line
3:00 3:30	Writing Progress Notes and Reading on Tourettes'	Counseling Ms. W.	Emergency Room Visit
4:00 4:30	Self-Esteem Group Session (6 Kids)	Agency Research Project (Reviewing Files)	Consultation with Jim C.'s Teacher
5:00			

FIGURE 7.1 Practicum reporting form

SOURCE: Adapted from Cooper, W. E. (1982). Time management techniques for clinicians. In P. A. Keller & L. G. Ritt (Eds.), *Innovations in clinical practice: A source book.* Sarasota, FL: Professional Resource Exchange.

A convenient way to determine what you have been learning in the agency is to review how you have spent your time. Agencies and social work programs use different procedures and forms to keep track of students' use of time. If, however, none is mandated and you are looking for a quick reporting scheme, see Figure 7.1 for an illustration of one that you could create for your own use.

Another variation would be to use a blank sheet of paper for each day you are in the practicum. Write down any cases, events, problems, or interesting situations you want to know more about. At the end of each week, you might want to write a summary of what you have learned. This information might be useful to you later when you prepare to enter the job market and need to create a resumé. But educationally, it is sound, too. Students often don't realize how much they have learned until they reflect back over their experiences.

Am I Permitted to Accumulate Overtime or Compensatory Time?

There may be occasions when you will be asked to work days or evenings beyond your scheduled time in the agency. The agency may experience a temporary staff shortage because of illness, vacations, or some other emergency. If you find yourself a few hours ahead in the work time you should have accumulated to that point, it would be appropriate to discuss with your field instructor whether to count these hours toward an earlier ending date for your practicum or whether you could be excused from one of your scheduled days in the agency.

It is not unusual for students to accumulate more hours in the practicum agency than they are required by their social work program. However, you should not plan to apply any excess hours in the current placement toward next semester's practicum. Although this might be allowed by some faculty field liaisons, it certainly is not an entitlement. You can see how the situation could get out of hand—especially if you changed agencies in the second practicum after accumulating 40 extra hours in the first practicum that you wanted to apply to the next agency. If you find yourself acquiring an excessive number of hours in your practicum, discuss this as soon as possible with your faculty field liaison.

How Do I Learn to Leave My Work at the Agency?

For your own mental health and well-being, do not take client and agency problems home with you. Concern yourself with clients' problems only when you are on duty at the agency. When you are at home or in the classroom, you need to give your attention to your family, friends, or schoolwork. Although it sounds a little callous, you do not own your clients' problems. You cannot "make" anyone get better. Although you will do your best to help, clients' problems are *their* problems. If you find yourself not sleeping or being preoccupied with a client's difficulties when you are at home or school, then you are probably overinvolved. If you suspect this might be true, then a discussion with your field instructor or faculty field liaison would be in order.

It will not always be easy to leave client problems at the agency at the end of the day. If you were not concerned about people, you probably wouldn't have chosen the career of social work. However, separating your work life from your leisure is a mental discipline that you must practice. To help you with this, make a personal rule to not bring paperwork from the agency home with you. Although it might be tempting to catch up on your progress notes or other work-related assignments at home, this is not advised. To do this type of work, client files or charts are usually needed, and students should never take agency files or confidential material out of the office without permission of the agency supervisor or field instructor. In one horror story, a student took several files home one evening only to have her briefcase containing the files stolen from her car. In another, a physician was taking home medical files, and the files actually blew out the window of his car and across the interstate highway.

What Do I Do if I Am Given Too Much or Too Little Responsibility?

Too much responsibility can be frightening! Overwhelming! A couple of years ago a student confided that in her placement, interns were assigned six or more cases the first day after orientation and told to schedule the appointments. They were expected to handle themselves as professionals, and if they needed help to ask for it. No help was given unless it was sought. Although the student's initial reaction was "poor me," by the end of her two semesters there she had been asked to remain as a paid employee. If, however, you feel as though you are being given too much to do, then you probably need to talk to your field instructor. Should that not work, then talk with your faculty field liaison.

If you are mildly concerned about what you perceive to be your unproven ability to help others, this probably would not be seen as a serious problem. On the other hand, if you are experiencing tremendous stress (e.g., insomnia, indigestion, panic attacks), then you likely are being given more responsibility than you can handle. In this instance, it is appropriate to inform your field instructor of what you are experiencing.

The problem of being given too little responsibility was addressed in Chapter 4. Briefly, students should expect to be occupied in direct service at least half of the time that they are in their placement. If this is not happening, talk first with the field instructor. If additional responsibilities are not given, then share your concerns with the faculty field liaison. All three participants in the learning contract (the student, the faculty field liaison, and the field instructor) need to be involved should problems arise in the practicum. Do not feel that you have to solve major problems in your field instruction by yourself.

What Do I Do When I Am Having a "Down" Day?

Sometimes the severity of clients' problems (e.g., child sexual abuse, adolescent suicide attempts, domestic violence) can cause students to experience "down" days—especially when a favorite client takes a turn for the worst (e.g., attempts suicide again or gets rearrested). Although intellectually students can tell themselves that it will be impossible to help every client, students are still likely to feel some pain when clients make bad choices for themselves.

It is important for you not to become depressed because of an action that a client freely chose. Do not label yourself as a failure if a client becomes dysfunctional. Almost always, clients have some problems in everyday functioning or they would not be requesting services from a social service agency. With problems such as substance abuse, it is expected that clients will "fall off the wagon" on one or more occasions even though they may later successfully maintain sobriety. One therapist's technique for avoiding depression when his clients had relapses was to think about the clients' strengths and then envision them using these assets at some future time to live successfully.

If you find yourself more than a little depressed or depressed fairly frequently because of the cases you have been assigned, tell your faculty field liaison. You may need therapy—particularly if these cases are close to some trauma you have personally experienced. If you find it too difficult to handle the emotional pain shared and experienced in the practicum setting, then you may be better suited for research or administrative social work than direct practice with clients.

What Do I Do When Things Are Not Going Well?

If agencies can be personified as people we know, some would be dynamic—fast moving, attractive, decisive. Others would have a frumpy appearance and would be slow moving and ponderous. Not every student can be placed in a dynamic agency. For one thing, there are probably too few of them and too many students. You know this intellectually and yet you are unhappy in your placement. When should you ask for another placement? Here are some suggested guidelines:

- When you are not getting adequate supervision (and you have repeatedly sought and requested it)
- When you are not being given anything to do, or when the work being given to you is clerical and you have made numerous requests for additional responsibility
- When you are being harassed or feel in danger
- When you discover that you cannot be empathic with persons you are assigned to counsel because of personal or traumatic experiences with this problem
- When you are required to be in the agency at a time when you are expected to be in class or at a field seminar, and the agency is inflexible in its demands
- When there is a significant personality clash between you and your agency supervisor (e.g., the supervisor gives the impression that you can do nothing right)
- When unethical or illegal practices are common occurrences (we will discuss ethics in more detail in Chapter 8)

Asking for another placement is not a decision to be taken lightly. This is especially true after you have spent four or five weeks in an agency. Some social work programs allow the student only one "replacement" in another setting. Nonetheless, some problems are so serious that students really ought to seek a new assignment—even if it means losing credit for the month spent in the first agency. Keep in mind, though, that it is not uncommon for students to experience a slow start—for field instructors to give very few assignments the first few weeks until they get to know the student and the student's capabilities. Sometimes the student feels that the first several weeks of a placement are spent reading with very little client contact.

There are logical explanations for this. Supervisors may want students to become more knowledgeable in a given area (e.g., the disease model of alcoholism) and may request completion of specific readings or observations before they assign clients. Supervisors may want to screen clients to ensure that the student is matched with one who can realistically show progress by the semester's end. Or, they may want to avoid assigning overly complicated cases to a student. Supervisors may want to wait for the "right" family before involving the student as a cotherapist. Furthermore, students may have to wait for sufficient clients to be recruited or identified before they can become involved as a group leader or coleader. Often there is little planning or recruiting for a new group until the student is established in the agency. So, expect some delays. Although it is frustrating, your agency supervisor will not always be available on a moment's notice. But none of these situations are by themselves good reasons for changing a practicum.

More serious concerns are when the agency is seriously mismanaged or understaffed, or when unethical practices are tolerated. In our program, a student interning in a group home for adolescents was made responsible for helping the residents prepare their meals over the weekend, but the only food left for her was a single can of lasagna. This event by itself was insufficient reason to remove a student, but it had been preceded by other indications of poor management. Hearing the student's account of this experience and then learning that the police were investigating one staff member for an illegal practice convinced us that the student would not have the type of experience that we had hoped. We moved the student to another agency.

Students should advocate for themselves—to try to rectify unhappy situations to the best of their abilities. When sincere (and usually repeated) effort has been made, then it is up to the faculty field liaison to decide the next course of action. Do not decide to leave an assignment without the approval of the faculty member who placed you there—this could result in a failing grade. What may seem to be an insurmountable problem to a student often turns out to be resolvable when a conscientious faculty member becomes involved.

If you spent a semester in a lackluster agency, or had a field instructor who contributed little to your educational experience, one way to feel better about this would be to discuss with your faculty field liaison the development or adoption of a student feedback form on field instructors, if one is not being used in your program. Feedback from students can improve the supervision and quality of future students' learning experiences by documenting when a particular field instructor performs unsatisfactorily.

How Do I Plan for My Next Practicum?

If you find yourself in a setting where your learning opportunities have been severely limited and you strongly feel that you need another practicum placement in a similar agency, then discuss this with your faculty field liaison. It would be to your advantage to give some thought to the areas of deficiency in this practicum setting and to the type of agency or program that could help you to develop needed skills. At some point in your practicum, you may learn of highly recommended agencies or field instructors from students who are farther along in the program than you are. Advocate for yourself sufficiently ahead of time so that your faculty field liaison can assign you to these agencies or with these field instructors.

Can a Friend Supervise Me?

Occasionally a student will discover that a friend has obtained a position in an agency and would be willing to provide supervision. As a rule, students should avoid seeking placements where friends, neighbors, family members, or others who might be less than objective would be the supervisor. Asking someone with whom you have a close relationship to supervise you likely would not be approved by your faculty field liaison and could get you into trouble if discovered later. For you to optimize your learning and grow professionally, it is necessary that your agency supervisor's objectivity not be impaired.

May I Audio- or Videotape Clients?

As part of your course work it may be required or desirable to reproduce one of your sessions with a client. Graybeal and Ruff (1995) have noted, "Audiotapes provide evidence of how much or little students talk, the modulation, tenor, and emotion of voice, and pace of interactions. Students and instructors can pick up on tones, attitudes, and subtleties not available in the written record" (p. 275). Videotape is even better because students and instructors can see body language and movement in the room as well as hear the dialogue with all its inflections.

Taping saves you the arduous task of remembering everything that happened in a session. If you are required by your faculty field liaison to tape a session with a client, do not assume that your agency supervisor will know about it. Discuss your need to audio or videotape a client with your agency supervisor. The two of you can then begin the necessary planning and client selection. Keep in mind, though, that you must *always* obtain the client's permission before you begin to audio- or videotape—even if the client's identity will not be known to your audience or identifiable characteristics can be obscured by editing. Most agencies require that clients indicate their agreement to taping by signing a written release or consent form. This is a good idea even if the agency does not have a prepared form. Most clients will not mind being taped and may be glad to help if you approach them in a straight-forward, honest, and relaxed manner. When you are interested in taping children, obtain permission from their parents or guardians.

Once permission has been secured, it is a good idea to test the equipment and make sure that you know how to operate the video or audio recorders. Experiment with the placement of the microphone or camera to ensure that you get the best possible recording. Have everything arranged so there will be minimal distraction or attention given to the equipment once the clients arrive. Do not remind clients to look toward the camera. Try to keep the equipment as unobtrusive as possible. Remember, the process of recording should be less important than what you and your clients achieve together in the session.

Afterwards, listen to or watch the tape critically. Analyze the material in terms of your feelings, thoughts, and the theoretical concepts you were employing. Make notes for discussion with your instructor. You may want to play back portions of the tape for the client to enable both parties to examine the helping process and to give the client an opportunity to comment on the intervention process.

Should I Share Personal Information with Clients?

In an effort to understand and relate to you, clients may ask personal questions such as, "Are you married?" "Do you have children?" "How old are you?" "How much do they pay you to do this?" If the student can share the information without feeling an invasion of privacy, then it is okay to answer such questions. Answer, if you can, in a brief and straightforward manner without comment about the meaning of the question. Such questions may be simple social curiosity. Sometimes, however, it is preferable to be a little vague in answering. In response to a question about his or her age, a student might reply, "I'm thirtyish."

Clients may ask about your experience because of a genuine interest in the helper's qualifications. Some clients may be reassured to know that you have completed courses in child development or that you will be completing your degree in May. Do not overexplain or become defensive. The client has a right to decide whether to continue with you or to ask for someone else. If you feel that the client is troubled by your lack of experience, ask, "Are you afraid that I won't be able to help you?" or, "Does this bother you?" Most clients will be so appreciative of someone assigned to help them that your qualifications will not be a major issue.

If you feel that a client's questions are a little too intrusive, you can deflect them by asking, "Why is that important to you?" or, "How does that relate to your purpose in coming here?" Generally, this will help clients to refocus on what they have come to the agency to obtain or accomplish.

Even though you may see no harm in answering a question about where you live, never give out your address or home phone number to clients without the knowledge of the field instructor. More than one student has been surprised when infatuated or disturbed clients have made unwanted and unanticipated visits to their apartments or homes. Also, nuisance phone calls are always a possibility when you give out your home phone number. Clients who may be suicidal or who may need to reach you in another emergency can call the agency's after-hours number, or you can direct them to call a 24-hour crisis counseling center until you can be reached again at the agency. (In extreme situations, the 24-hour crisis counseling center could be given your home phone number so that they could inform you when a client is having problems. You could return the client's call without the client learning your home phone number.)

Similarly, it is not advisable to correspond with active or former clients without your agency supervisor's knowledge, even if the clients are incarcerated and in another state. Although you may wish to correspond with a favorite client or an inmate out of concern or friendship, these situations can get misinterpreted and out of hand. Someone sitting in a jail cell all day with little to occupy his or her time may build elaborate fantasies and begin to see you in a way you had not intended.

Case Example

For your first practicum you are assigned to a residential facility for persons with developmental disabilities and mental retardation. After the second week, a friend stops by, and since you are not busy at the time, you take about 15 minutes to give your friend a tour of the facility. Later, the agency director makes it clear that you are not to invite friends and family members to the facility. You explain that you had not invited your friend; she had just shown up, and you were merely being polite. Your feelings are a little hurt.

The next weekend, the interior of the facility is being painted and all but about four clients go home for a visit. Jim, a long-time employee of the facility, has a visit from his girlfriend on Saturday afternoon. They go into the office and keep the door closed for about two hours. During this time Jim does not answer the phone or attend to any agency business that you can observe.

Questions

1. Should you inform your agency supervisor of Jim's activities?
2. Should you let Jim know that you felt that he was violating the rules?
3. Should you cover for Jim?

Am I Cut Out for Social Work?

From time to time even most seasoned professionals wonder if they have chosen the right vocation. Should you, too, be having some doubts, that is okay. Seldom does anyone have to make an immediate decision about a career choice. If your first practicum did not go well, this may not be a reflection on you. Perhaps your supervisor was too often unavailable or too critical. Maybe staff members just did not reach out to you because of internal strife or poor morale within the agency (e.g., frustration over lack of a pay raise). Despite your faculty field liaison's efforts, maybe your experience was not a pleasant one. Do not take this personally. Especially if you are not at the end of your social work program, most students will have another practicum to test whether social work is the right career.

Sometimes even a relatively unpleasant practicum yields useful learning about yourself or a certain population of clients. For instance, if you tend to be very trusting of people, you may have learned not to display that trait to drug addicts who are not very far along in their recovery process. Maybe this experience will direct you to another population (e.g., hospice patients) with whom you will build excellent rapport because of the same trait.

The purpose of the practicum is to provide you with the opportunity to learn experientially. Maybe there are some things you would do differently now. You do not have to consider changing careers even if you made a few mistakes in your practicum. (Of course, if these were serious mistakes, and you made several of them, this is a different matter.) Sometimes talking with your adviser or your faculty field liaison can help you evaluate the advantages and disadvantages of changing majors or careers.

Finally, if you felt that you did good work with your clients, be reassured by that. We do not always get recognized for a job well done. In fact, you are more likely to get recognition if you create a serious problem than if you handle your assignments effectively and efficiently.

What is Managed Care?*

You will hear the phrase "managed care" used in virtually every practicum setting. Managed care involves any kind of health or mental health services that are paid for by a third party (e.g., private insurance, Medicaid, or Medicare). The care is said to be managed

*The following five sections on managed care were written by Holly Riffe, Ph.D.

when some person other than the practitioner and client decides on the direction of the treatment (Shapiro, 1995). For example, prior to managed care, women would commonly stay in the hospital for at least two days after giving birth. With the advent of managed care, some insurance companies began insisting that the mother and baby be discharged in 24 hours. And, in community mental health centers, social workers may now be told by case managers to limit counseling to five sessions when clients have a diagnosis of depression.

The concept underlying managed care is cost containment. The costs of health care have skyrocketed over the past several decades and managed care has helped to stabilize costs; otherwise, insurance premiums would have increased much more than they have.

There are four main terms associated with managed care: (1) health maintenance organization, (2) preferred provider organization, (3) capitation, and (4) case management. A health maintenance organization (HMO) is a business that provides pre-paid comprehensive health care services. The easiest way to think about this is to envision a one-stop facility with a variety of practitioners like social workers, x-ray technicians, medical specialists, pharmacists, and physical therapists who provide services to patients of the HMO. The primary medical physician often determines which services will benefit the patient.

A Preferred Provider Organization (PPO) contracts with health care providers and hospitals within a community to provide services to their insured clients. This plan is similar to an HMO but instead of one building that houses all of the practitioners, the clinicians can be located anywhere in the community. The insured client's contract with the PPO will specify which specialty services are available through the network. For example, the PPO may allow the client to seek counseling from a social worker in the network for a predetermined number of sessions.

Capitation is when the insurance company pays a set fee in advance to the health care organization. That money is to be used to pay for any health needs of the group of people the company insures. If the providing organization does not use all of the money at the end of the year, then a profit is made; however, a deficit could be incurred if many of the insured required services or if those services were especially costly. Capitation creates a tremendous incentive for the practitioner to limit treatment to the least expensive options unless the cost of diseases such as AIDS and cancer are specifically included in the contract (James, 1996).

Case management is probably the most frequently encountered type of managed care for the social work practitioner. With certain forms of insurance, the social worker must negotiate with the insurance company's representative, often called a case manager, to determine what services the company will reimburse. For example, an insurance company may pay for a specified number of hospital days for a mastectomy. Sometimes the social worker must advocate for clients who need more services than that usually provided or reimbursed.

Where Should I Expect Managed Care?

Managed care is found in nearly all practice arenas where third party payers are involved. Social workers should be prepared to advocate for clients needing extended hospital stays or expensive treatments. When policies are unrealistic and detrimental to clients, you may have to become a broker for other services in order to compensate for shortened treatment in a hospital or inpatient facility. Home health care for medical services or community residential treatment for psychiatric patients may not be automatically provided or covered unless you request it. On a macro level, social workers may need to lobby for policies that will limit the influence of insurer's arbitrary decisions regarding clients' access to health and mental health care. For instance, Congress was responsible for extending the amount of time that new mothers and their babies could remain in the hospital.

How Does Managed Care Affect Practice?

Managed care affects social workers differently according to their practice fields. In medical social work, patients may be discharged from hospitals before they are able to take care of all of their daily needs. Social workers must take extra care in discharge assessments to ensure that patients have all the care that they need. Elderly clients may need home health nursing for a period of time to assist them in bathing or with wound care after surgery. High-risk infants may need to be seen by their pediatrician soon after returning home in order to be evaluated for certain life-threatening illnesses like metabolic disorders or respiratory ailments that were formerly monitored during hospitalization.

Managed care has had a significant impact on private counseling practices. Social workers are in competition with each other for insurance reimbursement and gather in large group practices to be attractive to insurers. They experience frustration when nurses or nonsocial workers in an office sometimes in another state decide—without even meeting their clients—how many counseling sessions the company will reimburse. Another irritant is that a tremendous amount of time-consuming paperwork has accompanied managed care and is necessary for reimbursement.

What Social Work Skills Are Important in a Managed Care Environment?

Advocacy. The major difficulty most clients have in a managed care system is the limitation placed on needed services. The social worker must advocate on behalf of clients for more hospital days, new or experimental treatments, additional services, or expensive medications.

Coalition building. When access to the best care is denied to patients, social workers can work to form coalitions with other service providers to apply pressure to insurers to extend and modify their policies.

Brokering. When the client's insurance refuses to pay for needed treatment, the social worker is obligated to look for other community resources that will be able to provide services to improve the client's quality of life.

How is Assessment Different in a Managed Care Environment?

With the emphasis on shorter treatment durations, the assessment process becomes increasingly critical. The social worker must hone in on the targeted problem and rapidly determine if there is a potential for danger to self or others. Assessment of clients' needs must be clearly documented and professionally written statements of fact. Callahan (1996) emphasizes that such records are now used to demonstrate that the social worker has adhered to a commonly accepted standard of care and, more importantly, to show that the clinician was not negligent if that case winds up in the legal system—which can sometimes happen when clients are harmed by not getting needed care or not getting it within a reasonable amount of time.

Clients are often evaluated with what is called biopsychosocial assessment. In the "bio" section, the practitioner reviews any physical problems that could influence functioning. For instance, a person with diabetes may act "strangely" when his or her blood sugar fluctuates. The psychological assessment focuses primarily on symptoms described in the Diagnostic and Statistical Manual (DSM-IV) and how those characteristics impact the client's daily life. Depression may cause a person to lose weight and have little interest in the activities of daily life. The final section details all the social influences in a person's life including relationships with significant others, co-workers, family, and friends. Sometimes it might be helpful for students to construct an eco-map to get a visual picture of all of the relationships and the energy exchange involved in the client's life (Hartman & Laird, 1983).

Finally, social workers must remember that the use of collateral information becomes increasingly important in documenting the need for extended care and for protection from litigation (Rey, 1996). The social worker must show that historical records were not only requested but also consulted in formulating the new treatment plan. Clients' reports of their past histories are no longer sufficient unless, of course, the client refuses to give permission for the social worker to review past charts or to speak with family members. If the records indicate that the client has been violent or suicidal in the past, then the clinician's argument to extend treatment will be received more positively than if that information was not known.

How Do I Prepare for Social Work Practice in the Next Century?

As we approach the twenty-first century, it is natural to speculate about how things might be different in a few years and how that may affect the practice of social work. As a student who wants to be well prepared for practicing in the future, you may wish to keep the following populations and trends in mind as you look for and negotiate a field placement.

- The elderly (those 65 and older) will constitute a significant proportion of the population and the old-old (those who are 85 and older) will be a substantial proportion of the elderly population. More and more of these elderly will be healthy and active and living in the community, but requiring services to assist them with living independently.

- The proportion of nonwhites in the population will continue to grow. Hispanics will add more people to the population than any other group. Asians will be another fast-growing racial/ethnic group. Knowledge of Spanish will be an asset for many social work practitioners.
- Poverty, with all its power to generate numerous other problems, will continue to plague large sections of the population. The faces of poverty will stay essentially the same. This population will need the same services and resources provided today.
- Violence in our homes and on our streets will continue to characterize our culture, and we will continue to see the casualties of that violence in cases of elder, spouse, and child abuse. The search will continue for more effective ways of remediation. The field of criminology will likely employ more social workers.
- Physical, social, psychological, and emotional problems attributable to lifestyle, environment, substance abuse, and stress will continue to grow in number and complexity. There will be a need for creative and imaginative interventions.
- In all areas of human services, much more emphasis will be placed on prevention and early detection. Social workers will need to become more proactive in their interventions.
- Greater use of technology in all sectors will deemphasize some of the traditional social work roles but at the same time create new and innovative roles. Scientific advances, particularly in medicine and genetics, will create challenging ethical questions.
- Computer technology will pervade all dimensions of life. Social service agencies will face even greater requirements for accountability and evaluation of efforts. Many more jobs for evaluation specialists and information managers will develop. Further, clients may be monitored to a much greater extent than they are presently; case management may focus on "likely" or predicted needs given the analysis of prior patterns and "typical" client profiles.

Ideas for Enriching the Practicum Experience

1. Begin to reflect on your experience thus far in the practicum. What would you say is the most important thing that you learned from working with the clients? What is the most important thing that you learned from working with staff members? Did you accomplish everything that you set out to learn in your learning contract? What do you still need to learn in the next practicum?
2. Consider what you have learned from this practicum and this academic term and then review your résumé. What might you change in the way you describe or present yourself?
3. Overall, how would you evaluate the agency and the program to which you were assigned? Would you recommend it to other students? Why or why not?
4. If there are similar programs in the community, schedule a visit to learn how they provide services. Do they use the same intake procedures or different ones? Do they provide intervention about the same way as your agency does? Have they conducted any evaluative research on the effectiveness of their program?

References

Callahan, J. (1996). Documentation of client dangerousness in a managed care environment. *Health & Social Work, 21*(3), 202–207.

Cooper, W. E. (1982). Time management techniques for clinicians. In P. A. Keller & L. G. Ritt (Eds.), *Innovations in clinical practice: A source book* (pp. 177–183). Sarasota, FL: Professional Resource Exchange.

Gibelman, M. & Schervish, P. H. (1996). The private practice of social work: Current trends and projected scenarios in a managed care environment. *Clinical Social Work Journal, 24*(3), 323–338.

Graybeal, C. & Ruff, E. (1995). Process recording: It's more than you think. *Journal of Social Work Education, 31,* 169–181.

Hartman, A., & Laird, J. (1983). *Family centered social work practice.* New York: Free Press.

James, J. S. (1996). Growing crisis in paying for care. In *AIDS Treatment News,* Issue 241 [On Line]. <http://www.immunet.org/immunet/atn.nsf/pagea-241-03> February 16, 1996.

Rey, L. D. (1996). What social workers need to know about client violence. *Families in Society: The Journal of Contemporary Human Services, 77,* 33–39.

Shapiro, J. (1995). The downside of managed mental health care. *Clinical Social Work Journal, 24*(3), 323–338.

Additional Readings

Dhooper, S. S. (1997). *Social Work in health care in the 21st century.* Thousand Oaks, CA: Sage.

Chapter **8**

Legal and Ethical Concerns

Overview

This chapter discusses professional boundaries, ethical responsibilities, and legal liability.

What Happens if I Make a Mistake?

It is hard to go through life (or maybe even a week) without making some kind of a blunder. What happens if you make a mistake in your practicum? First, let's examine several examples of small mistakes:

1. You have promised a client that you would obtain information about a community resource and you forgot to do so.
2. While interviewing a client, you forget an important question you had intended to ask.
3. You fail to get a client's signature on a necessary form.

These problems are not serious because each can be easily resolved by a phone call or at the time of the client's next visit.

Most mistakes that you make as a student probably will not involve legal or ethical considerations. However, some mistakes are more serious than others. For example, you might inadvertently disclose confidential information about a client receiving services to someone whom the client did not want to know. Or, you might not take action to protect someone threatened by the client you counsel twice a week. In instances where something you have done or failed to do results in harm or could have resulted in injury, where a complaint could or might be filed against the agency, you should inform your field instructor as soon as possible.

Minor mistakes may cause some inconvenience (e.g., a client having to make another trip to the agency to sign a form), but major mistakes violate rights or have the potential to cause harm. Always inform your field instructor about major mistakes, but it is not necessary to mention every little oversight. When in doubt, it is better to inform your field instructor than to treat the mistake as a secret.

Case Example

Carrie was assigned to escort a nursing home patient with dementia through a series of diagnostic tests at a large university hospital. While waiting for the lab to draw the patient's blood, Carrie momentarily left Mr. Jones in a wheel chair to make a phone call. When she returned, the patient was gone. Three hours later the patient was found huddled in a corner of the hospital's basement. Because he was unhurt, Carrie doesn't think she needs to inform the nursing home staff about the patient's disappearance.

Questions

1. Does Carrie have an obligation to inform the nursing home?
2. Would Carrie have less of an obligation to inform the nursing home if the patient had been lost for only 45 minutes?

What is Malpractice?

Malpractice is defined as an act of commission or omission by a professional that falls below accepted standards of care and results in or aggravates an injury to the client. Students in field placements are acting in a professional role which involves the responsibility to uphold the same professional, legal and ethical standards as other practicing social workers. Clients expect students to perform their role in a competent manner. However, students are vulnerable to the extent that they lack professional skills.

Zakutansky and Sirles (1993) have listed several examples of situations that can lead to civil or criminal action against a student. These include:

misrepresenting qualifications, such as failing to inform the client of student status; providing treatment without obtaining proper consent; keeping inaccurate or inadequate records; administering inappropriate or radical treatment; failing to consult with or refer to a specialist; failing to seek proper supervision; failing to take action to prevent a client's suicide; and failing to warn third parties of potential harm. (p. 340)

Can Confidential Client Material Ever Be Shared?

Most social work students, by the time they are ready to start a practicum, have been well drilled on the importance of respecting confidentiality. From the NASW Code of Ethics (reprinted as Appendix B), students have learned to hold in confidence information obtained in the course of professional service. You've learned that you need explicit written permission of a client to share information about them with anyone other than the professional staff of the agency. And you've learned that the NASW Code of Ethics states that clients should have access to records concerning them; that care should be taken to protect the confidences of others contained in those records; and that the social worker should obtain the informed consent of clients before taping, recording, or permitting third-party observation of their activities.

By the start of the practicum, students have also learned that the term *confidentiality* in a social service agency generally refers to relative confidentiality, not absolute confidentiality. The Federal Privacy Act of 1974 makes it clear that information about clients and staff may be shared with officers and employees of the agency who need such records in the performance of their duties. That information revealed by a client can be subpoenaed for use in court also helps students to understand the concept of relative confidentiality.

Unquestionably, there are times when information obtained from clients should be shared with others. The client's right to confidentiality, for instance, does not extend to the abuse or harm of children. All 50 states have statutes that require professionals to report any suspected child abuse or neglect. In some states, professionals are also required to report elder abuse. Similarly, if a client makes a serious threat of suicide, or harm to others, this information should be shared with other professionals and family members even if it violates confidentiality.

Guidelines for violating the client's confidentiality are not well defined. For instance, if a client threatens a criminal act (e.g., a man says he is going to beat his partner), professionals must weigh the seriousness of the crime and abandon the principle of confidentiality to prevent serious harm. Using this criterion, illegal activities such as buying or selling marijuana do not justify breaking confidentiality. Engaging in prostitution does not either, unless the individual is infected with AIDS. When confronted with a dilemma about breaching a client's confidentiality, it is always important to discuss your next course of action with your agency supervisor. Certainly, disclosure without a client's permission should take place only under the most extreme circumstances and only as a last resort (Reamer, 1991).

Relative confidentiality can also be seen in the way that researchers, evaluators, and quality assurance personnel read case records or parts of these records to determine which clients are benefiting from intervention, and the characteristics of clients enrolled in selecting programs. Generally, clients must give their permission in order to participate in a research or evaluation project. However, if the nature of the research or evaluation relies on closed cases or historical data, then client permission generally is not sought, provided that personal identifying information (e.g., the client's name, address, or phone number) is not recorded and that the research methodology does not involve contacting clients directly.

Occasionally, social work students may be asked to make a case presentation to one of their classes or seminars. In such situations, sharing details of a case is not a violation of the client's confidentiality if you do not give out any personal identifying information. However, do not describe clients in such a way that they can be recognized. Instead, be somewhat general in your description and try to change a few personal details. You might say, for instance, that the client is a 40-year-old mother of four with a professional career, who has been referred from the courts for a first-time shoplifting offense. If you find it necessary to refer to the client by a name, make one up or refer to the client by some initial (e.g., "Mrs. B").

Descriptions that could fit any number of people in the community because they do not identify the client are not a violation of clients' confidentiality when used within a professional or educational context. However, the more times you repeat a description, the greater the likelihood that someone might recognize your client. For this reason, professionalism requires that even brief, general descriptions of clients not be shared at parties and social occasions.

The same discretion is expected if you should identify a client from another student's presentation. Occasionally during classes or seminars, a client who receives services from more than one agency will be recognized by one or more students who know each other. Whenever this happens, you are bound by the same principle of confidentiality as is the student assigned the case and making the presentation.

Confidentiality is a complex subject that can be covered only superficially in this section. You may want to consult additional readings (Abramson, 1990; Alperin, 1989; Jacobs, 1991; Lindenthal, Jordan, Lentz, & Thomas, 1988; Reamer, 1991; Schwartz, 1989; Watkins, 1989). You also would be well advised to ask your field instructor about the agency's policies regarding confidentiality and what you should tell clients about protecting what they tell you in confidence. Clients should be informed about the limits of confidentiality before, rather than after, they disclose information that could result in their arrest.

Do I Need Liability Insurance?

The United States is a very litigious society. Social workers and social work agencies are not immune from being sued for malpractice. Kurzman (1995) has given several reasons for this including: (1) in all 50 states social work has gained legal stature and its practice is regulated by law; (2) courts are less likely to grant protection from liability; (3) there is an easy availability of negligence attorneys willing to work on a contingency basis; and (4) changes in liability associated with managed care.

Although the chances of a social work student being sued are small, the expense of defending against even a preposterous charge can quickly go beyond the resources of most students. Having liability insurance does not protect you from being sued. However, if you are sued, the insurance will be greatly appreciated.

Only a few social work programs provide liability insurance for students. Some programs require their students to purchase this insurance. In most programs, students have the option of purchasing liability insurance. Should you buy liability insurance if it is not required? The best argument for buying the insurance is that the National Association of Social Workers Insurance Trust offers it at a relatively inexpensive rate.

Another argument for purchasing the insurance would be if you are placed in an agency where there have been recent suits against staff members or where you feel that conditions are right for a suit against an employee or the agency. On the other hand, you may be provided some protection by the agency's or even the university's liability policy. However, you cannot always count on this. You can be sued as an individual. Protection that you think you have under the agency's policy might evaporate if attorneys for the agency argue that you were not a bona fide employee. If you can spare the cash, purchasing liability insurance is worthwhile, although it is unlikely that you will ever use it.

What is an Ethical Dilemma?

An ethical dilemma is when you must make a choice among arguably correct but conflicting courses of action. Dilemmas also usually involve negative repercussions either for you or the client. The following list from Blumenfield & Lowe (1987) identifies situations where ethical dilemmas may be experienced. Such circumstances include:

- Conflict between one's personal and professional values
- Conflict between two values/ethical principles
- Conflict between two possible actions, each with reasons strongly favorable and unfavorable
- Conflict between two unsatisfactory alternatives
- Conflict between one's values/principles and one's perceived role
- Conflict between the need to act and the need to reflect

To further illustrate how it is possible to be caught in an ethical dilemma, consider the following example:

You are interning as a school social worker, and your first day in the school your field instructor is out sick. The principal is juggling several crises and asks you to help out by meeting with a nine-year-old who has been crying since arriving at school that morning.

The child is very reluctant to talk, but you coax and encourage. Finally, the child says that she'll tell you, but only if you promise to tell no one else what she reveals. In your haste to learn what has been troubling her, you agree. The child then divulges a history of abusive treatment by her stepmother.

By law you are required to report known or suspected incidents of child abuse. Further, the principal and the child's homeroom teacher are both interested in her welfare and want you to share what you have learned. However, you made a promise. Do you break your promise and inform the child protection authorities and the principal? If you break your promise, will that destroy the rapport you have established with the child? If the abuse cannot be substantiated by child protection services (CPS), will the nine-year-old receive worse treatment at home as a result of your reporting the stepmother?

Can Ethical Dilemmas Be Avoided?

The social work intern in the above scenario created a difficult situation by promising to hold the nine-year-old's story confidential. The dilemma could have been avoided if the social work student had not promised to safeguard the nine-year-old's account. A better way to have handled this would have been to show concern, reiterate to the child that no one has a right to hurt or threaten her, communicate that you want to help *but* that the law requires you to share information with other people under certain circumstances. In other words, you would inform the client early on, before anything important has been revealed, of your professional obligation to report child abuse.

At the same time, it is entirely possible that informing a child of the necessity to report any abuse may result in the child clamming up and not talking any further with you. The child may need to meet with you on several occasions before she trusts you enough to reveal anything important.

So, while the ethical dilemma might have been avoided in this first example, it is very unlikely that you will be able to practice social work without encountering others. For instance, suppose you are running a self-esteem group in a high school. During an especially productive session a 16-year-old student reveals that since he broke up with his girlfriend, he has been smoking pot and doing other drugs. He wants help, but he also does not want his parents to know. His father is the chief of police.

Is the student the only client? Should the parents also be viewed as the client system? Should they be informed that their son is breaking the law? Does the principal have a right to know that the student is bringing marijuana onto school property and may be selling it to classmates?

Because most students are minors, it is unclear in many situations whether information about a child should be transmitted to the parents or kept confidential. In this second scenario, however, the intern should urge the client to stop bringing illegal drugs onto campus and to disclose to his parents his need for substance abuse counseling. Many social workers feel that confidentiality should extend to minors as well as to adults; they also believe that advising them to disclose important information is consistent with the social work value of client self-determination.

Because of advances in technology and its ability to sustain life of those in frail health, social workers in medical settings can also expect to have to deal with complex ethical problems. In these settings the social worker may discover conflicts when multiple parties (the patient's family, the hospital, and even society—which wants scarce medical resources justly allocated) each have different visions of what is best for the patient.

A recent study of hospital social workers (Proctor, Morrow-Howell, & Lott, 1993) found that the majority of ethical conflicts they reported consisted of a clash between the client's self-determination and what social workers judged not to be in the client's best interest. For example, the patient wants to be discharged, but he or she would not accept the amount of in-home help needed to live independently. In 61 percent of the social workers' cases, there was some disagreement among parties about discharge destination.

Can ethical dilemmas be completely avoided? Probably not. It is best to prepare yourself for them by examining your own values from time to time and learning all you can about how past ethical problems in your practicum setting were resolved.

How Do I Avoid Rushing into Ethical Dilemmas?

Two actions are helpful in keeping ethical dilemmas at arm's length: first, develop a working knowledge of the NASW Code of Ethics, reprinted in Appendix B. The Code of Ethics provides general guidelines for ethical behavior. These standards may not, however, suggest what you should do in every instance. By necessity they cannot be specific to every possible ethics violation. At the same time, some behaviors will almost always be viewed as unethical. These include such behaviors as:

- Sexual intimacy with clients
- Libeling or slandering a client
- Sharing confidences without compelling professional reasons
- Assaulting, causing physical injuries, or placing clients in danger
- Dishonesty, fraud, or misrepresentation

Printed with the premission of Chris Rosenthal

- Discriminatory practices
- Withdrawing services precipitously (abandoning a client)
- Failure to warn and protect the victim of a violent crime
- Failure to exercise reasonable precautions with a potentially suicidal client
- Promising "cures" for problems

Second, you can avoid ethical dilemmas by anticipating likely trouble spots before they occur. If, for instance, your practicum is in a school, you should give prior thought to how you would respond if a child reveals abuse or neglect. Find out how your field instructor wants you to handle these situations. What information does the school expect you will share with concerned teachers? The principal?

Additionally, be alert to areas where your values may collide with the clients' best interest. For example, if you believe that keeping families together is the most important thing you can do as a social worker, you may not be as quick to recognize the emotional damage occurring within a family when an abuser lives there and doesn't cooperate with counseling. In one real life situation a father with explosive anger kicked in his ten year-old child's bedroom door because the parent wanted to punish his son for coming home a few minutes late for supper. When the worried mother got on the phone and called the "family counselor," he did not encourage her to call the police or the child protection authorities—actions that would have resulted in greater protection of the child and the mother and probably would have provided the motivation for the father to participate in therapy.

Case Example

Retta is an undergraduate student in a practicum at a large, multi-service agency with strict eligibility standards based on income. Retta has a client, Tonya, a single mother with four small children, who is struggling to get by on her welfare check. Tonya also receives a small amount of assistance with her large utility bill from the agency. However, Retta receives a phone call from Tonya's neighbor informing her that Tonya has been working part time and not reporting her income.

Questions

1. Should Retta just forget about this piece of information and allow Tonya to provide more income for her family?
2. Should Retta reduce the amount of assistance by the income the neighbor reported? What would you do?
3. Could the "correct" response for Retta to make be in opposition to the most ethical course of action?

How Do I Resolve Ethical Dilemmas?

The first step in resolving an ethical dilemma is recognizing the problem and identifying the source of the conflict. For instance, is it a clash between professional and personal values? Between professional values and agency policy? It may be useful to write down the problem as you understand it and then to gather relevant information. How has this problem been handled in the past?

You also must keep all parties informed of your legal and ethical obligations. Engage clients or involved parties in dialogue, and brainstorm the "best" course of action. Make sure you are constantly keeping in mind the mission of the profession and observing the client's right to self-determination. If you are still unclear about what to do, discuss the situation with your field instructor or faculty liaison. Protect the identity of the client if necessary, and present the situation as a "hypothetical" case.

Lowenberg and Dolgoff (1996) have suggested an approach for ordering social work values that might help you get off the "horns of a dilemma." For instance, they say that protection of life should always take precedence over lower-ranked values, such as privacy and confidentiality, or even truthfulness (as when you have to break a promise). Their priority ranking of ethical principles is as follows:

1. Protection of life
2. Equality
3. Autonomy and freedom
4. Least harm
5. Quality of life
6. Privacy and confidentiality
7. Truthfulness and full disclosure

How do you know when you are doing the right thing? It is not always possible to know, but there is a greater chance that we can feel good about the decision we have to make if we go through a deliberate process where we examine our values, seek additional information, and consult others.

Joseph (cited in Garrett, 1994) has outlined a decision-making model that requires these steps: (1) definition of the dilemma, (2) looking at all the relevant facts and developing valid arguments for various courses of action, (3) consideration of practice wisdom, personal beliefs and values, and how these might influence the final decision, (4) developing options, exploring compromises, evaluating alternatives in an attempt to find a course of action with the least negative effects, and (5) choosing a position that you can defend.

Other decision-making models have been discussed by Lowenberg and Dolgoff (1996) and Tymchuck (1992). When you have conscientiously gone through such a process to resolve ethical dilemmas, then you have done all that can be done.

Case Example

Freda and Holly are placed in a large agency where their field instructor is so busy that she scarcely has time to see them each week. Mrs. Morgan, the field instructor, had agreed to accept the two students before she learned that she would be given responsibility for managing a new branch office miles from town. Because she is frequently unavailable to them, Freda and Holly have been using their time in the practicum setting to do their homework and catch up on reading for their other courses. After the first month, Freda and Holly have yet to see a client, and they have only been given some basically clerical assignments like answering the phones and finding files.

Freda wants to inform their faculty liaison that they are not being used appropriately and are not learning any social work skills. Holly says, "Why ruin a good thing?" She clearly communicates that she will be most unhappy if Freda speaks to their faculty liaison.

Questions
1. Should Freda take the chance that things will eventually settle down for Mrs. Morgan and that she will find some meaningful assignments for them before the semester is out?
2. Should Freda go against her friend's wishes and speak to Mrs. Morgan or their faculty liaison? What are the arguments for each position?
3. Besides speaking to Mrs. Morgan or their faculty liaison, what else could Freda do to enrich her own experience within the agency?

May I Accept a Gift from a Client?

Sometimes clients are so appreciative that they want to give their favorite social worker a gift. Some agencies have policies on receiving gifts; others do not. Check with your agency supervisor if a client hints that he or she will be bringing you a present. The client's giving of a small gift may be a demonstration of simple gratitude for being helpful or for simply accepting something that the client said or did. But the gift may also be an attempt to ask the therapist to like the client more, or to manipulate the therapist (Gabel, Oster, & Pfeffer, 1988). This would be particularly true with expensive or extravagant gifts. In the absence of an agency policy, you may want to devise one of your own— such as not accepting gifts valued at more than ten dollars. Generally, small tokens of appreciation, such as cookies, a small painting, or a ceramic creation made by the client, can be graciously accepted.

> Cynthia received a birthday card from a client who had heard a couple of staff talking about taking her out for lunch. When Cynthia opened the card, she found a $50 bill in it. That night in her practicum group she revealed that she didn't know what to do. The client was on probation and she was afraid that if she told her field instructor, the client would get into trouble. She wanted to return the money quietly without informing her supervisor. Without exception, her classmates strongly urged her not to keep it secret but to advise the field instructor. Otherwise, they reasoned, the client might accuse Cynthia of taking a bribe or soliciting favors.

Once in a while, a client will want to give a special student a gift even after a case has been transferred or closed. Generally when this happens, there is some dependency on the client's part and the client may be trying to keep the student involved in the case. If it is a small gift, it may be possible to accept it. However, you may want to have the client leave the gift at the agency or with another worker, so that you can pick it up without becoming entangled again.

Is it Ever Permissible to Date Clients or Coworkers?

Students should not date clients or socialize with them outside of the agency. Although one date may not lead to romantic involvement, in any dating situation where there is physical attraction the potential for sexual involvement exists. And it is never permissible for helping professionals to engage in sexual activities with their clients. The NASW Code of Ethics (1996) states, "Social workers should under no circumstances engage in sexual activities or sexual contact with current clients." Further, social workers are prohibited from engaging in sexual activities with clients' relatives or other individuals with whom clients maintain close personal relationships when there is risk of harm to the client. In fact, because of its destructive consequences for clients, all of the major mental health professions have explicit prohibitions against therapist–client sexual involvement. In some states legislation has been passed making therapist–client sexual intimacy a criminal offense.

If you find that you are strongly attracted to a client, the advised course of action is to speak to your agency supervisor about arranging a transfer of this client to another staff member. Romantic involvement jeopardizes professional objectivity. The social worker's judgment about what is best for the client may be clouded as the social worker becomes overprotective and overinvolved.

Confine relationships with patients to the office, except when specific interventions are needed elsewhere. When would it be appropriate to see a client outside of the office? An example would be when it is impossible to talk or hear in your office (e.g., because of remodeling or construction), and it is convenient to walk to the corner restaurant and talk over coffee or a soft drink. In such instances, inform at least one other person in the agency (e.g., your agency supervisor) of your whereabouts. Although it is clear that, given a choice, some clients may prefer not to meet in the office, the use of an office within an established agency lends an air of propriety. Requests from clients to meet outside of the office may indicate an interest in manipulating or undercutting progress being made.

It also is not a good idea to date staff members within the agency as long as you are a student there. When there are breakups, relationships have a way of causing hard feelings. Former soul-mates can turn vindictive or uncooperative. Even if the relationship doesn't turn sour, you might not be able to maximize your learning in an agency where your relationship becomes a prime topic of conversation and office relationships are extremely difficult to keep secret. Finally, the NASW Code of Ethics (1996) states:

> Social workers who function as supervisors or educators should not engage in sexual activities or contact with supervisees, students, trainees, or other colleagues over whom they exercise professional authority.

What Do I Do if I Observe Something Illegal or Unethical?

It is possible that you will observe or overhear something in an agency that strikes you as illegal or unethical. Consider this example: A student intern observes an employee apparently stealing an assortment of office supplies. Should the student report this to her field instructor? Probably not. The employee may be working at home on agency-related work and plans on bringing the unused materials back to the office the next morning. It is not the student's role to police other employees.

However, if you were to observe someone in the agency misappropriating client funds, fondling a client, or snorting drugs, then you would have a responsibility to report these much more serious accusations to your field instructor. The NASW Code of Ethics (1996) requires social workers who have a direct knowledge of a social work colleague's impairment due to personal problems, substance abuse, or mental difficulties to take action through appropriate channels.

Sometimes it is very difficult to know whether some action should be reported. One student was told not to use the agency phone for personal calls, yet observed a staff member who tied up a phone line for 45 minutes on a call to her boyfriend. This was not fair, and the student wanted to complain to her field instructor. In fact, she did complain. The field instructor took no action. The staff member was a personal friend of the field instructor, and there was no disciplinary action. But the student was viewed as a malcontent who was always complaining. Her final evaluation was much lower than her midterm evaluation.

The best advice is to consider the seriousness of the offense or charge. Is someone harmed or likely to be harmed? Contemplate what the consequences would be if you are wrong. What if you were mistaken and the 45-minute call was not to a boyfriend but to a legitimate client who was falling apart and needed 45 minutes of the social worker's time? If you are sure that you are right and the charge is serious enough to be unethical, illegal, or unprofessional, then discuss the incident in private with your field instructor or your faculty field liaison, and the two of you can decide what the next step should be.

How Do I Handle Agency Secrets?

Once in a while students learn of transactions or behaviors within an agency that are not common knowledge. For instance, the treasurer may have been accused of embezzling a sum of money or the director may have been sued for palimony. Because the agency is not your client, you are not obligated to keep this information confidential in the same way as you have to safeguard sensitive material that clients share with you. However, you would be well advised to be very discreet in revealing these agency secrets.

For one thing, the allegations could turn out to be completely false and the result of vicious rumor. It would be embarrassing (if not irresponsible) if you were to spread such gossip throughout the community. Could you be guilty of slander in this situation? Furthermore, the personal affairs of agency officials may not interfere with their administrative abilities within the agency. Airing an agency's secrets in public could contribute to the agency's loss of reputation in the community and do a disservice to the many fine, hard-working, and unselfish staff members.

If you feel that the private information that you have about the agency has or could have a direct effect on the quality of services to clients or the learning in your practicum, then report this information to either your field instructor or your faculty field liaison. Also report this information if you think it might prevent future students from being placed in the agency. Otherwise, whom you tell about the agency's secrets depends on your own discretion.

How Do I Handle Sexual Harassment?

Sexual harassment is unwanted verbal or physical conduct of a sexual nature. This includes compliments of a very personal or sexual nature, pressure for dates or sexual contact, jokes with suggestive themes, unwelcome notes, or physical activities such as touching, brushing against, unsolicited back rubs, or blocking passage with one's body. The few studies available on sexual harassment of social workers have shown that human service agencies are not immune from this problem and that almost 30 percent of social workers have experienced some form of sexual harassment.

When does a hug or a touch become sexual harassment? Sexual harassment is one-sided. There is no reciprocity involved; the offender's behavior is unwelcome and almost always repetitive. A single incident usually is not sexual harassment unless a serious threat or assault is involved.

Another aspect of sexual harassment is that the offender may use clout or power of position to insinuate that the victim has much to lose by not going along with the offender's requests. Sexual harassment exists when you fear a loss of position or status, or negative evaluation, because you rejected sexual advances. Both men and women can be victims of sexual harassment.

If you feel that you are being subjected to sexual harassment, you should immediately inform your primary supervisor. If the person harassing you is the supervisor, or if you do not feel comfortable discussing the matter with this person, then by all means contact your faculty field liaison. Often, the situation will not improve until someone—

the victim—decides to take a stand. One of our graduate students, placed in a psychiatric setting, was repeatedly subjected to derogatory comments from a male physician about the nature of her work. These comments were completely unfounded and sexist in nature. When the student discussed this situation with her field instructor, a great deal of support was generated for her, and the result was that a letter of disciplinary action was placed in the physician's personnel folder.

Do not be silent just because you are a student or because you don't have much longer in the placement. If you are feeling sexually harassed, it is likely that the same offender is harassing others. There are laws to protect you against sexual harassment. One way to avoid becoming a victim is to familiarize yourself with your agency's policies for complying with sexual harassment laws. Dhooper, Huff, and Schultz (1989) found that 54 percent of social workers surveyed were ignorant of the applicable laws.

Ideas for Enriching the Practicum Experience

1. Interview staff at your practicum agency about ethical dilemmas they have encountered over the years.
2. Read one of the suggested references at the end of this unit and draw up a list of questions for class discussion.
3. Read the NASW Code of Ethics (reprinted in Appendix B) and highlight any areas that are not clear to you. Discuss these either with your field instructor or in class.
4. Compare the NASW Code of Ethics with the latest American Psychological Association ethics code or the American Medical Association's ethics code. Where do the different codes overlap? Where do they differ?

References

Abramson, M. (1990). Keeping secrets: Social workers and AIDS. *Social Work, 35*(2), 169–173.

Alperin, D. E. (1989). Confidentiality and the BSW field work placement process. *Journal of Social Work Education, 25*(2), 98–108.

Blumenfield, S., & Lowe, J. I. (1987). A template for analyzing ethical dilemmas in discharge planning. *Health and Social Work, 12*(1), 47–56.

Dhooper, S. S., Huff, M. B. & Schultz, C. M. (1989). Social work and sexual harassment. *Journal of Sociology and Social Welfare, 16*(3), 125–138.

Dolgoff, R., & Skolnik, L. (1992). Ethical decision making, the NASW Code of Ethics and group work practice: Beginning explorations. *Social Work with Groups, 15*(4), 99–112.

Gabel, S., Oster, G., & Pfeffer, C. R. (1988). *Difficult moments in child psychiatry.* New York: Plenum Medical.

Garrett, K. J. (1994). Caught in a bind: Ethical decision making in schools. *Social Work in Education, 16*(2), 97–105.

Jacobs, C. (1991). Violations of the supervisory relationship: An ethical and educational blind spot. *Social Work, 36*(2), 130–135.

Kurzman, P. A. (1995). Professional liability and malpractice. In *Encyclopedia of Social Work,* 19th Edition, Washington, D.C.: National Association of Social Workers, pp. 1921–1927.

Lindenthal, J. J., Jordan, T. J., Lentz, J. D. & Thomas, C. S. (1988). Social workers' management of confidentiality. *Social Work, 33*(2), 157–159.

Lowenberg, F. M., & Dolgoff, R. (1996). *Ethical decisions for social work practice.* Itasca, IL: Peacock.

National Association of Social Workers. Code of Ethics (1996). Washington, D.C., National Association of Social Workers.

Proctor, E. K., Morrow-Howell, N., & Lott, C. L. (1993). Classification and correlates of ethical dilemmas in hospital social work. *Social Work, 38*(2), 166–177.

Reamer, F. G. (1991). AIDS, social work, and the "duty to protect." *Social Work, 36*(1), 56–60.

Schwartz, G. (1989). Confidentiality revisited. *Social Work, 34*(3), 223–226.

Tymchuck, A. J. (1992). Strategies for resolving value dilemmas. *American Behavioral Scientist, 26*(2), 159–175.

Watkins, S. A. (1989). Confidentiality and privileged communications: Legal dilemma for family therapists. *Social Work, 34*(2), 133–136.

Zakutansky, T. J., & Sirles, E. A. (1993). Ethical and legal issues in field education: Shared responsibility and risk. *Journal of Social Work Education, 29,* 338–347.

Additional Readings

Alexander, R., Jr. (1993). The legal liability of social workers after DeShaney. *Social Work, 38,* 64–68.

Cobb, N. H. (1994). Court-recommended guidelines for managing unethical students and working with university lawyers. *Journal of Social Work Education, 30,* 18–31.

Congress, E. P., & Chernesky, R. H. (1993). Representative payee programs for the elderly: Administrative, clinical, and ethical issues. *Journal of Gerontological Social Work, 21*(1/2), 77–93.

Corey, G., Corey, M., & Callanan, P. (1988). *Issues and ethics in the helping professions.* Pacific Grove, CA: Brooks/Cole.

Davidson, J. R., & Davidson, T. (1996). Confidentiality and managed care: Ethical and legal concerns. *Health & Social Work, 21,* 208–215.

Gelman, S. R., & Wardell, P. J. (1988). Who's responsible? The field liability dilemma. *Journal of Social Work Education, 24*(1), 70–78.

Howling, P. T. & Wodarski, J. S. (1992). Legal requisites for social workers in child abuse and neglect situations. *Social Work, 37,* 330–335.

Hutchinson, E. D. (1993). Mandatory reporting laws: Child protective case finding gone awry. *Social Work, 38,* 56–63.

Jacobs, C. (1991). Violations of the supervisory relationship: An ethical and educational blind spot. *Social Work, 36,* 130–135.

Kagle, J. D. & Giebelhausen, P. N. (1994). Dual relationships and professional boundaries. *Social Work, 39,* 213–220.

Kagle, J. D., & Kopels, S. (1994). Confidentiality after Tarasoff. *Health & Social Work, 19,* 217–222.

Kopels, S., & Kagle, J. D. (1993). Do social workers have a duty to warn? *Social Service Review, 67*(1), 10–26.

Kugelman, W. (1992). Social work ethics in the practice arena: A qualitative study. *Social Work in Health Care, 17*(4), 59–77.

Kutchins, H. (1991). The fiduciary relationship: The legal basis for social workers' responsibilities to clients. *Social Work, 36*(2), 106–113.

Loewenberg, F., & Dolgoff, R. (1996). *Ethical decisions for social work practice.* Itasca, IL: F. E. Peacock.

MacKay, E., & O'Neill, P. (1992). What creates the dilemma in ethical dilemma? Examples from psychological practice. *Ethics & Behavior, 2*(4), 227–244.

Rhodes, M. L. (1986). *Ethical dilemmas in social work practice.* London: Routledge & Kegan Paul.

Wells, C. C., & Masch, M. K. (1986). *Social work ethics day to day: Guidelines for professional practice.* New York: Longman.

Appendix **A**

Problem-Oriented Recording

Record-keeping today involves a complex series of decisions in which social work agencies have to balance the costs of detailed reporting systems against their benefits. How much information and what information should become part of the official record? What information is pertinent and what is immaterial? More comprehensive records generally allow greater accountability but are costlier to maintain and may provide less protection of the client's confidentiality.

Information in ongoing records must be organized in some logical, coherent manner, and social service agencies have tackled this problem in several ways. One approach, the problem-oriented record (also known as the problem-oriented medical record, the problem-goal-oriented record, the problem-oriented system, or Weed system), has been widely adopted by agencies in health and human service settings. This approach has been described as having a "remarkable concurrence with and support of social work principles and functions" (Biagi, 1977, p. 212).

The problem-oriented record has four components: (1) a data base that contains relevant information about the client; (2) a problem list that includes a statement of initial complaints; (3) an assessment and plan related to each identified problem; and (4) progress notes about what was done and the outcome of each activity.

There are several variations of the problem-oriented record. Perhaps the most often used form is **SOAP**. For each identified problem, the social worker records *subjective* information (the client's perception of the problem), *objective* information (the facts of the case; information that can be verified), the *assessment* (the professional's conclusions about the nature of the problem), and the *plan* for intervention. Another variation is **PAP** (*problem, assessment, plan*), in which the client's subjective complaint and the objective information pertaining to the problem are brought together. The assessment and plan portions of PAP remain the same as in SOAP.

Tremendous diversity exists in social service agencies, particularly in how they are organized and run. In fact, the way in which your practicum agency wants you to record client data in its files may not look at all like the SOAP or PAP systems. Sometimes other organizational schemes form the basis for documenting pertinent client information in the agency's records. For instance, some of the data may be organized using Perlman's (1957) *4-Ps* (*person, problem, place,* and *process*) or Doremus's (1976) *4-Rs* (*roles, reactions, relationships,* and *resources*). You may discover many variations of these schemes as you are placed in different social service agencies.

To help you visualize what the problem-oriented record would look like, we have taken the same case example and presented it first in a SOAP format, then in a PAP framework.

Example of Problem-Oriented Medical Record Subjective and Objective Information, Assessment, Plan (SOAP)

Data Base:

Mrs. B., a 60-year-old widowed female, was admitted reporting headaches, dizziness, unsteady gait, double vision, and episodes of forgetfulness. She was diagnosed as having an aneurysm. After surgery, she had partial right eye vision loss, and right side paralysis. Patient has a tenth-grade education, has worked as a hotel maid until recently. She has no children or close relatives. Says that her religion is very important to her.

Problem #1: Anxiety Over Disability

Subjective:

"I'm so nervous; my nerves are shot—worrying about how I'm going to manage with one good arm and leg. I've got so many questions rattling around inside of me sometimes I think I'm going to explode. I can't get a straight answer out of them doctors."

Objective:

The ruptured aneurysm and resulting surgery have left Mrs. B. with serious disabilities that will likely keep her from working again. Medical staff may have presented too optimistic a picture prior to surgery and not prepared her sufficiently for the condition in which she now finds herself.

Assessment:

Patient is having a difficult time adjusting to her partial paralysis. She is concerned that she might not be allowed to return to her own home. Additionally, patient will be unable to work and will experience a loss of income. Both of these fears are well founded in reality, although if patient makes good progress in physical therapy there is no reason she couldn't return home, although she may require some assistance, at least initially.

Plan:

1. Encourage Mrs. B. to ventilate her feelings.
2. Provide Mrs. B. with emotional support and help her use her religious faith in dealing with the situation.
3. Involve medical staff in clarifying her physical status and prognosis.
4. Encourage patient to continue with physical therapy and make plans for the future.
5. Help client apply for disability.

Problem #2: Need for Post-Hospital Care

Mrs. B. will not be able to live independently in her apartment in her present condition and does not want to go to a nursing home, even temporarily.

Subjective:

"There's no way I could get up into bed by myself, or go down into the basement to wash a load of clothes. Why, I've never used my left hand for anything—now I'm going to have to use it for everything. How am I going to tie my shoes?"

Objective:

Patient does not ambulate at this time, but seems to be making good use of her left hand to feed self, answer the phone, etc. A rehab hospital can help patient with her walking, and introduce her to appliances that will facilitate her living independently. Whether she will regain use of her right hand is questionable.

Assessment:

Patient needs intensive physical therapy at a rehabilitative hospital in order to learn how to live with significant disabilities. Her concerns about self-care are real. Patient's physician agrees that Mrs. B. can benefit from intensive rehabilitation and has requested a consult from Cardinal Valley Hospital.

Plan:

1. Discuss with patient the need for a referral to a rehabilitation hospital.
2. Arrange for the patient to visit the rehab hospital.
3. Prepare the patient psychologically for changes in her life caused by the paralysis.
4. Talk with Mrs. B. about other alternatives (in-home assistance) in the event that she can't get into the rehab hospital immediately.
5. Complete the discharge plan and application process to rehab hospital.

Example of Problem-Oriented Medical Record
Problem, Assessment, Plan (PAP)

Data Base:

Mrs. B., a 60-year-old widowed female, was admitted reporting headaches, dizziness, unsteady gait, double vision, and episodes of forgetfulness. She was diagnosed as having an aneurysm. After surgery, she had partial right eye vision loss, and right side paralysis. Patient has a tenth-grade education, has worked as a hotel maid until recently. She has no children or close relatives. Says that her religion is very important to her.

Problem #1: Anxiety of Disability

Mrs. B. worries about her inability to get around and feels that she has been given ambivalent messages about the extent or recovery she can expect.

Assessment:

Patient is having a difficult time adjusting to her partial paralysis. She is concerned that she might not be allowed to return to her own home. Additionally, patient will be unable to work and will experience a loss of income.

Plan #1:

1. Encourage Mrs. B. to ventilate her feelings.
2. Provide Mrs. B. with emotional support and help her use her religious faith in dealing with the situation.
3. Involve medical staff in clarifying her physical status and prognosis.
4. Encourage patient to continue with physical therapy.
5. Help patient apply for disability.

Problem #2: Need for Post-Hospital Care

Mrs. B. will not be able to live independently in her apartment in her present condition and does not want to go to a nursing home, even temporarily.

Assessment:

Patient needs intensive physical therapy at a rehabilitative hospital and must learn to adjust to life with a significant disability.

Plan #2:

1. Discuss with patient the need for a referral to a rehabilitation hospital.
2. Arrange for the patient to visit the rehab hospital.
3. Prepare the patient psychologically for changes in her life caused by the paralysis.
4. Talk with Mrs. B. about other alternatives (in-home assistance) in the event that she can't get into the rehab hospital immediately.
5. Complete the discharge plan and application process to rehab hospital.

References

Biagi, E. (1977). The social work stake in problem-oriented recording. *Social Work in Health Care, 3*(2), 211–221.

Doremus, B. (1976). The four R's: Social diagnosis in health care. *Health and Social Work, 23*(July), 296–299.

Perlman, H. (1957). *Social casework: A problem-solving process.* Chicago: University of Chicago Press.

Additional Readings

Burke, P. C. (1988). Consultation and the use of policy guidelines in case recording. *Social Work Education, 7*(3), 7–11

Hartman, B. L., & Wickey, J. M. (1978). The person-oriented record in treatment. *Social Work, 23*(July), 296–299.

Johnson H. C. (1978). Integrating the problem-oriented record with a systems approach to case assessment. *Journal of Education for Social Work, 14*(3) 71–77.

Kagle, J. D. (1993). Record-Keeping: Directions for the 1990s. *Social Work, 38*(2), 190–196.

Kane, R. A. (1974). Look to the record. *Social Work 19*(4), 412–419.

Vickar, G. M., & Herjanic, M. (1976). The use of problem-oriented medical records in community mental health centers. *American Journal of Psychiatry, 133*(3), 340–341.

Weed, L. L. (1969). *Medical records, medical education and patient care.* Cleveland, OH: Case Western Reserve University.

National Association of Social Workers Code of Ethics (1996)

The following ethical standards are relevant to the professional activities of all social workers. These standards concern (1) social workers' ethical responsibilities to clients, (2) social workers' ethical responsibilities to colleagues, (3) social workers' ethical responsibilities in practice settings, (4) social workers' ethical responsibilities as professionals, (5) social workers' ethical responsibilities to the social work profession, and (6) social workers' ethical responsibilities to the broader society.

Some of the standards that follow are enforceable guidelines for professional conduct, and some are aspirational. The extent to which each standard is enforceable is a matter of professional judgment to be exercised by those responsible for reviewing alleged violation of ethical standards.

1. Social Workers' Ethical Responsibilities to Clients

1.01 Commitment to Clients

Social workers' primary responsibility is to promote the well-being of clients. In general, clients interests are primary. However, social workers' responsibility to the larger society or specific legal obligations may on limited occasions supersede the loyalty owed clients, and clients should be so advised. (Example include when a social worker is required by law to report that a client had abused a child or has threatened to harm self or other.)

1.02 Self-Determination

Social workers respect and promote the right of clients to self-determine and assist clients in their efforts to identify and clarify their goals. Social workers may limit clients' right to self-determination when, in the social workers' professional judgment, clients' actions or potential actions pose a serious, foreseeable, and imminent risk to themselves or others.

1.03 Informed Consent

(a) Social workers should provide services to clients only in the context of a professional relationship based, when appropriate, on valid informed consent. Social workers should

133

use clear and understandable language to inform clients of the purpose of the services, risks related to the services, limits to services because of the requirements of a third-party payer, relevant costs, reasonable alternatives, clients' right to refuse or withdraw consent, and the time frame covered by the consent. Social workers should provide clients with an opportunity to ask questions.

(b) In instances when clients are not literate or have difficulty understanding the primary language used in the practice setting, social workers should take steps to ensure clients' comprehension. This may include providing clients with a detailed verbal explanation or arranging for a qualified interpreter or translator whenever possible.

(c) In instances when clients lack the capacity to provide informed consent, social workers should protect clients' interests by seeking permission from an appropriate third party, informing clients consistent with the clients' level of understanding. In such instances social workers should seek to ensure that the third party acts in a manner consistent with clients' wishes and interests. Social workers should take reasonable steps to enhance such clients' ability to give informed consent.

(d) In instances when clients are receiving services involuntarily, social workers should provide information about the nature and extent of services and about the extent of clients' right to refuse service.

(e) Social workers who provide services via electronic media (such as computer, telephone, radio, and television) should inform recipients of the limitations and risks associated with such services.

(f) Social workers should obtain clients' informed consent before audiotaping or videotaping clients or permitting observation of services to clients by a third party.

1.04   Competence

(a) Social workers should provide services and represent themselves as competent only within the boundaries of their education, training, license, certification, consultation received, supervised experience, or other relevant professional experience.

(b) Social workers should provide services in substantive areas or use intervention techniques or approaches that are new to them only after engaging in appropriate study, training, consultation, and supervision from people who are competent in those interventions or techniques.

(c) When generally recognized standards do not exist with respect to an emerging area of practice, social workers should exercise careful judgment and take responsible steps (including appropriate education, research, training, consultation, and supervision) to ensure the competence of their work and to protect the clients from harm.

1.05   Cultural Competence and Social Diversity

(a) Social workers should understand culture and its function in human behavior and society, recognizing the strengths that exist in all cultures.

(b) Social workers should have a knowledge base of their clients' cultures and be able to demonstrate competence in the provision of services that are sensitive to clients' cultures and to differences among people and cultural groups.

(c) Social workers should obtain education about and seek to understand the nature of social diversity and oppression with respect to race, ethnicity, national origin, color, sex, sexual orientation, age, marital status, political belief, religion, and mental or physical disability.

1.06   Conflict of Interest

(a) Social workers should be alert to and avoid conflicts of interest that interfere with the exercise of professional discretion and impartial judgment. Social workers should inform clients when a real or potential conflict of interest arises and take reasonable steps to resolve the issue in a manner that makes the clients' interests primary and protects clients' interests to the greatest extent possible. In some cases, protecting clients' interests may require termination of the professional relationship with proper referral of the client.

(b) Social workers should not take unfair advantage of any professional relationship or exploit others to further their personal, religious, political, or business interests.

(c) Social workers should not engage in dual or multiple relationships with clients or former clients in which there is a risk of exploitation or potential harm to the client. In instances when dual or multiple relationships are unavoidable, social workers should take steps to protect clients and are responsible for setting clear, appropriate, and culturally sensitive boundaries. (Dual or multiple relationships occur when social workers relate to clients in more than one relationship, whether professional, social, or business. Dual or multiple relationships can occur simultaneously or consecutively.)

(d) When social workers provide services to two or more people who have a relationship with each other (for example, couples, family members), social workers should clarify with all parties which individuals will be considered clients and the nature of social workers' professional obligations to the various individuals who are receiving services. Social workers who anticipate a conflict of interest among the individuals receiving services or who anticipate having to perform in potentially conflicting roles (for example, when a social worker is asked to testify in a child custody dispute or divorce proceedings involving clients) should clarify their roles with the parties involved and take appropriate action to minimize any conflict of interest.

1.07   Privacy and Confidentiality

(a) Social workers should respect the clients' right to privacy. Social workers should not solicit private information from clients unless it is essential to providing services or conducting social work evaluation or research. Once private information is shared, standards of confidentiality apply.

(b) Social workers may disclose confidential information when appropriate with valid consent from a client or a person legally authorized to consent on behalf of a client.

(c) Social workers should protect the confidentiality of all information obtained in the course of professional service, except for compelling professional reasons. The general expectation that social workers will keep information confidential does not apply when disclosure is necessary to prevent serious, foreseeable, and imminent harm to a client or other identifiable person or when laws or regulations require disclosure without a client's consent. In all instances, social workers should disclose the least amount of confidential information necessary to achieve the desired purpose; only information that is directly relevant to the purpose for which the disclosure is made should be revealed.

(d) Social workers should inform clients, to the extent possible, about the disclosure of confidential information and the potential consequences, when feasible before the disclosure is made. This applies whether social workers disclose confidential information on the basis of a legal requirement or client consent.

(e) Social workers should discuss with clients and other interested parties the nature of confidentiality and limitations of clients' right to confidentiality. Social workers should review with clients circumstances where confidential information may be requested and where disclosure of confidential information may be legally required. This discussion should occur as soon as possible in the social worker-client relationship and as needed throughout the course of the relationship.

(f) When social workers provide counseling services to families, couples, or groups, social workers should seek agreement among the parties involved concerning each individual's right to confidentiality and obligation to preserve the confidentiality of information shared by others. Social workers should inform participants in family, couples, or group counseling that social workers cannot guarantee that all participants will honor such agreements.

(g) Social workers should inform clients involved in family, couples, marital, or group counseling of the social worker's, employer's, and agency's policy concerning the social worker's disclosure of confidential information among the parties involved in the counseling.

(h) Social workers should not discuss confidential information to third-party payers unless clients have authorized such disclosure.

(i) Social workers should not disclose confidential information in any setting unless privacy can be ensured. Social workers should not discuss confidential information in public or semipublic areas such as hallways, waiting rooms, elevators, and restaurants.

(j) Social workers should protect the confidentiality of clients during legal proceedings to the extent permitted by law. When a court of law or other legally authorized body orders social workers to disclose confidential or privileged information without a client's consent and such disclosure could cause harm to the client, social workers should request that the court withdraw the order or limit the order as narrowly as possible or maintain the records under seal, unavailable for public inspection.

(k) Social workers should protect the confidentiality of clients when responding to requests from members of the media.

(l) Social workers should protect the confidentiality of clients' written and electronic records and other sensitive information. Social workers should take reasonable steps to ensure that clients' records are stored in a secure location and that clients' records are not available to others who are not authorized to have access.

(m) Social workers should take precautions to ensure and maintain the confidentiality of information transmitted to other parties through the use of computers, electronic mail, facsimile machines, telephones and telephone answering machines, and other electronic or computer technology. Disclosure of identifying information should be avoided whenever possible.

(n) Social workers should transfer or dispose of clients' records in a manner that protects clients' confidentiality and is consistent with state statutes governing records and social work licensure.

(o) Social workers should take reasonable precautions to protect client confidentiality in the event of the social worker's termination of practice, incapacitation, or death.

(p) Social workers should not disclose identifying information when discussing clients for teaching or training purposes unless the client has consented to disclosure of confidential information.

(q) Social workers should not disclose identifying information when discussing clients with consultants unless the client has consented to disclosure of confidential information or there is a compelling needs for such disclosure.

(r) Social workers should protect the confidentiality of deceased clients consistent with the preceding standards.

1.08   Access to Records
(a) Social workers should provide clients with reasonable access to records concerning the clients. Social workers who are concerned that clients' access to their records

could cause serious misunderstanding or harm to the client should provide assistance in interpreting the records and the consultation with the client regarding the records. Social workers should limit clients' access to their records, or portions of their records, only in exceptional circumstances when there is compelling evidence that such access would cause serious harm to the client. Both clients' requests and the rationale for withholding some or all of the records should be documented in clients' files.

(b) When providing clients with access to their records, social workers should take steps to protect the confidentiality of other individuals identified or discussed in such records.

1.09   Sexual Relationships

(a) Social workers should under no circumstances engage in sexual activities or sexual contact with current clients, whether such contact is consensual or forced.

(b) Social workers should not engage in sexual activities or sexual contact with clients' relatives or other individuals with whom clients maintain a close personal relationship when there is a risk of exploitation or potential harm to the client. Sexual activity or sexual contact with clients' relatives or other individuals with whom clients maintain a personal relationship has the potential to be harmful to the client and may make it difficult for the social worker and client to maintain appropriate professional boundaries. Social workers—not their clients, their clients' relatives, or other individuals with whom the client maintains a personal relationship—assume the full burden for setting clear, appropriate, and culturally sensitive boundaries.

(c) Social workers should not engage in sexual activities or sexual contact with former clients because of potential for harm to the client. If social workers engage in conduct contrary to this prohibition or claim that an exception to this prohibition is warranted because of extraordinary circumstances, it is social workers—not their clients—who assume the full burden of demonstrating that the former client has not been exploited, coerced, or manipulated, intentionally or unintentionally.

(d) Social workers should not provide clinical services to individuals with whom they have had a prior sexual relationship. Providing clinical services to a former sexual partner has the potential to be harmful to the individual and is likely to make it difficult for the social worker and individual to maintain appropriate professional boundaries.

1.10   Physical Contact

Social workers should not engage in physical contact with clients when there is a possibility of psychological harm to the client as a result of the contact (such as cradling or caressing clients). Social workers who engage in appropriate physical contact with clients are responsible for setting clear, appropriate, and culturally sensitive boundaries that govern such physical contact.

1.11   Sexual Harassment

Social workers should not sexually harass clients. Sexual harassment includes sexual advances, sexual solicitation, requests for sexual favors, and other verbal or physical conduct of a sexual nature.

1.12   Derogatory Language

Social workers should not use derogatory language in their written or verbal communications to or about clients. Social workers should use accurate and respectful language in all communications to and about clients.

1.13   Payment for Services

(a) When setting fees, social workers should ensure that the fees are fair, reasonable, and commensurate with the services performed. Consideration should be given to clients' ability to pay.

(b) Social workers should avoid accepting goods or services from clients as payment for professional services. Bartering arrangements, particularly involving services, create the potential for conflicts of interest, exploitation, and inappropriate boundaries in social workers' relationships with clients. Social workers should explore and may participate in bartering only in very limited circumstances when it can be demonstrated that such arrangements are an accepted practice among professionals in the local community, considered to be essential for the provision of services, negotiated without coercion, and entered into at the client's initiative and with the client's informed consent. Social workers who accept goods or services from clients as payment for professional services assume the full burden of demonstrating that this arrangement will not be detrimental to the client or the professional relationship.

(c) Social workers should not solicit a private fee or other remuneration for providing services to clients who are entitled to such available services through the social workers' employer or agency.

1.14   Clients Who Lack Decision-Making Capacity

When social workers act on behalf of clients who lack the capacity to make informed decisions, social workers should take reasonable steps to safeguard the interests and rights of those clients.

1.15   Interruption of Services

Social workers should make reasonable efforts to ensure continuity of services in the event that services are interrupted by factors such as unavailability, relocation, illness, disability, or death.

1.16   Termination of Services

(a) Social workers should terminate services to clients and professional relationships with them when such services and relationships are no longer required or no longer serve the clients' needs or interests.

(b) Social workers should take reasonable steps to avoid abandoning clients who are still in need of services. Social workers should withdraw services precipitously only under unusual circumstances, giving careful consideration to all factors in the situation and taking care to minimize possible adverse effects. Social workers should assist in making appropriate arrangements for continuation of services when necessary.

(c) Social workers in fee-for-service settings may terminate services to clients who are not paying an overdue balance if the financial contractual arrangements have been made clear to the client, if the client does not pose an imminent danger to self or others, and if the clinical and other consequences of the current nonpayment have been addressed and discussed with the client.

(d) Social workers should not terminate services to pursue a social, financial, or sexual relationship with a client.

(e) Social workers who anticipate the termination or interruption of services to clients should notify clients promptly and seek the transfer, referral, or continuation of services in relation to the clients' needs and preferences.

(f) Social workers who are leaving an employment setting should inform clients of appropriate options for the continuation of services and of the benefits and risks of the options.

2. Social Workers' Ethical Responsibilities to Colleagues

2.01 Respect

(a) Social workers should treat colleagues with respect and should represent accurately and fairly the qualifications, views, and obligations of colleagues.

(b) Social workers should avoid unwarranted negative criticism of colleagues in communications with clients or with other professionals. Unwarranted negative criticism may include demeaning comments that refer to colleagues' level of competence or to individuals' attributes such as race, ethnicity, national origin, color, sex, sexual orientation, age, marital status, political belief, religion, and mental or physical disability.

(c) Social workers should cooperate with social work colleagues and with colleagues of other professions when such cooperation serves the well-being of clients.

2.02 Confidentiality

Social workers should respect confidential information shared by colleagues in the course of their professional relationships and transactions. Social workers should ensure that such colleagues understand social workers' obligation to respect confidentiality and any exceptions related to it.

2.03 Interdisciplinary Collaboration

(a) Social workers who are members of an interdisciplinary team should participate in and contribute to decisions that affect the well-being of clients by drawing on the perspectives, values, and experiences of the social work profession. Professional and ethical obligations of the interdisciplinary team as a whole and of its individual members should be clearly established.

(b) Social workers for whom a team decision raises ethical concerns should attempt to resolve the disagreement through appropriate channels. If the disagreement cannot be resolved, social workers should pursue other avenues to address their concerns consistent with client well-being.

2.04 Disputes Involving Colleagues

(a) Social workers should not take advantage of a dispute between a colleague and an employer to obtain a position or otherwise advance the social workers' own interests.

(b) Social workers should not exploit clients in disputes with colleagues or engage clients in any inappropriate discussion of conflicts between social workers and their colleagues.

2.05 Consultation

(a) Social workers should seek the advice and counsel of colleagues whenever such consultation is in the best interests of clients.

(b) Social workers should keep themselves informed about colleagues' areas of expertise and competencies. Social workers should seek consultation only from colleagues who have demonstrated knowledge, expertise, and competence related to the subject of the consultation.

(c) When consulting with colleagues about clients, social workers should disclose the least amount of information necessary to achieve the purposes of the consultation.

2.06 Referral for Services

(a) Social workers should refer clients to other professionals when the other professionals' specialized knowledge or expertise is needed to serve clients fully or when social workers believe that they are not being effective or making reasonable progress with clients and that additional service is required.

(b) Social workers who refer clients to other professionals should take appropriate steps to facilitate an orderly transfer of responsibility. Social workers who refer clients to other professionals should disclose, with clients' consent, all pertinent information to the new service providers.

(c) Social workers are prohibited from giving or receiving payment for a referral when no professional service is provided by the referring social worker.

2.07 Sexual Relationships

(a) Social workers who function as supervisors or educators should not engage in sexual activities or contact with supervisees, students, trainees, or other colleagues over whom they exercise professional authority.

(b) Social workers should avoid engaging in sexual relationships with colleagues when there is potential for a conflict of interest. Social workers who become involved in, or anticipate becoming involved in, a sexual relationship with a colleague have a duty to transfer professional responsibilities, when necessary, to avoid a conflict of interest.

2.08 Sexual Harassment

Social workers should not sexually harass supervisees, students, trainees, or colleagues. Sexual harassment includes sexual advances, sexual solicitation, requests for sexual favors, and other verbal or physical conduct of a sexual nature.

2.09 Impairment of Colleagues

(a) Social workers who have direct knowledge of a social work colleague's impairment that is due to personal problems, psychosocial distress, substance abuse, or mental health difficulties and that interferes with practice effectiveness should consult with that colleague when feasible and assist the colleague in taking remedial action.

(b) Social workers who believe that a social work colleague's impairment interferes with practice effectiveness and that the colleague has not taken adequate steps to address the impairment should take action through appropriate channels established by employers, agencies, NASW, licensing and regulatory bodies, and other professional organizations.

2.10 Incompetence of Colleagues

(a) Social workers who have direct knowledge of a social work colleague's incompetence should consult with that colleague when feasible and assist the colleague in taking remedial action.

(b) Social workers who believe that a social work colleague is incompetent and has not taken adequate steps to address the incompetence should take action through appropriate channels established by employers, agencies, NASW, licensing and regulatory bodies, and other professional organizations.

2.11 Unethical Conduct of Colleagues

(a) Social workers should take adequate measures to discourage, prevent, expose, and correct the unethical conduct of colleagues.

(b) Social workers should be knowledgeable about established policies and procedures for handling concerns about colleagues' unethical behavior. Social workers should be familiar with national, state, and local procedures for handling ethics complaints. These include policies and procedures created by NASW, licensing and regulatory bodies, employers, agencies, and other professional organizations.

(c) Social workers who believe that a colleague has acted unethically should seek resolution by discussing their concerns with the colleague when feasible and when such discussion is likely to be productive.

(d) When necessary, social workers who believe that a colleague has acted unethically should take action through appropriate formal channels (such as contacting a state licensing board or regulatory body, an NASW committee on inquiry, or other professional ethics committees).

(e) Social workers should defend and assist colleagues who are unjustly charged with unethical conduct.

3. Social Workers' Ethical Responsibilities in Practice Settings

3.01 Supervision and Consultation

(a) Social workers who provide supervision or consultation should have the necessary knowledge and skill to supervise or consult appropriately and should do so only within their areas of knowledge and competence.

(b) Social workers who provide supervision or consultation are responsible for setting clear, appropriate, and culturally sensitive boundaries.

(c) Social workers should not engage in any dual or multiple relationships with supervisees in which there is a risk of exploitation of or potential harm to the supervisee.

(d) Social workers who provide supervision should evaluate supervisees' performance in a manner that is fair and respectful.

3.02 Education and Training

(a) Social workers who function as educators, field instructors for students, or trainers should provide instruction only within their areas of knowledge and competence and should provide instruction based on the most current information and knowledge available in the profession.

(b) Social workers who function as educators or field instructors for students should evaluate students' performance in a manner that is fair and respectful.

(c) Social workers who function as educators or field instructors for students should take reasonable steps to ensure that clients are routinely informed when services are being provided by students.

(d) Social workers who function as educators or field instructors for students should not engage in any dual or multiple relationships with students in which there is risk of exploitation or potential harm to the student. Social work educators and field instructors are responsible for setting clear, appropriate, and culturally sensitive boundaries.

3.03 Performance Evaluation

Social workers who have responsibility for evaluating the performance of others should fulfill such responsibility in a fair and considerate manner and on the basis of clearly stated criteria.

3.04 Client Records

(a) Social workers should take reasonable steps to ensure that documentation in records is accurate and reflects the services provided.

(b) Social workers should include sufficient and timely documentation in records to facilitate the delivery of services and to ensure continuity of services provided to clients in the future.

(c) Social workers' documentation should protect clients' privacy to the extent that is possible and appropriate and should include only information that is directly relevant to the delivery of services.

(d) Social workers should store records following the termination of services to ensure reasonable future access. Records should be maintained for the number of years required by state statutes or relevant contracts.

3.05 Billing

Social workers should establish and maintain billing practices that accurately reflect the nature and extent of services provided and that identify who provided the service in the practice setting.

3.06 Client Transfer

(a) When an individual who is receiving services from another agency or colleague contacts a social worker for services, the social worker should carefully consider the client's needs before agreeing to provide services. To minimize possible confusion and conflict, social workers should discuss with potential clients the nature of the clients' current relationship with other service providers and the implications, including possible benefits or risks, of entering into a relationship with a new service provider.

(b) If a new client had been served by another agency or colleague, social workers should discuss with the client whether consultation with the previous provider is in the client's best interest.

3.07 Administration

(a) Social work administrators should advocate within and outside their agencies for adequate resources to meet client's needs.

(b) Social workers should advocate for resource allocation procedures that are open and fair. When not all clients' needs can be met, an allocation procedure should be developed that is nondiscriminatory and based on appropriate and consistently applied principles.

(c) Social workers who are administrators should take reasonable steps to ensure that adequate agency or organizational resources are available to provide appropriate staff supervision.

(d) Social work administrators should take reasonable steps to ensure that the working environment for which they are responsible is consistent with and encourages compliance with the *NASW Code of Ethics*. Social work administrators should take reasonable steps to eliminate any conditions in their organizations that violate, interfere with, or discourage compliance with the *Code*.

3.08 Continuing Education and Staff Development

Social work administrators and supervisors should take reasonable steps to provide or arrange for continuing education and staff development for all staff for whom they are responsible. Continuing education and staff development should address current knowledge and emerging developments related to social work practice and ethics.

3.09 Commitments to Employers

(a) Social workers generally should adhere to commitments make to employers and employing organizations.

(b) Social workers should work to improve employing agencies' policies and procedures and the efficiency and effectiveness of their services.

(c) Social workers should take reasonable steps to ensure that employers are aware of social workers' ethical obligations as set forth in the *NASW Code of Ethics* and of the implications of those obligations for social work practice.

(d) Social workers should not allow an employing organization's policies, procedures, regulations, or administrative orders to interfere with their ethical practice of social work. Social workers should take reasonable steps to ensure that their employing organizations' practices are consistent with the *NASW Code of Ethics*.

(e) Social workers should act to prevent and eliminate discrimination in the employing organization's work assignments and in its employment policies and practices.

(f) Social workers should accept employment or arrange student field placements only in organizations that exercise fair personnel practices.

(g) Social workers should be diligent stewards of the resources of their employing organizations, wisely conserving funds where appropriate and never misappropriating funds or using them for unintended purposes.

3.10 Labor-Management Disputes

(a) Social workers may engage in organized action, including the formation of and participation in labor unions, to improve services to clients and working conditions.

(b) The actions of social workers who are involved in labor-management disputes, job actions, or labor strikes should be guided by the profession's values, ethical principles, and ethical standards. Reasonable differences of opinion exist among social workers concerning their primary obligation as professionals during an actual or threatened labor strike or job action. Social workers should carefully examine relevant issues and their possible impact on clients before deciding on a course of action.

4. Social Workers' Ethical Responsibilities as Professionals

4.01 Competence

(a) Social workers should accept responsibility or employment only on the basis of existing competence or the intention to acquire the necessary competence.

(b) Social workers should strive to become and remain proficient in professional practice and the performance of professional functions. Social workers should critically examine and keep current with emerging knowledge relevant to social work. Social workers should routinely review the professional literature and participate in continuing education relevant to social work practice and social work ethics.

(c) Social workers should base practice on recognized knowledge, including empirically based knowledge, relevant to social work and social work ethics.

4.02 Discrimination

Social workers should not practice, condone, facilitate, or collaborate with any form of discrimination on the basis of race, ethnicity, national origin, color, sex, sexual orientation, age, marital status, political belief, religion, or mental or physical disability.

4.03 Private Conduct

Social workers should not permit their private conduct to interfere with their ability to fulfill their professional responsibilities.

4.04 Dishonesty, Fraud, and Deception

Social workers should not participate in, condone, or be associated with dishonesty, fraud, or deception.

4.05 Impairment

(a) Social workers should not allow their own personal problems, psychosocial distress, legal problems, substance abuse, or mental health difficulties to interfere with their professional judgment and performance or to jeopardize the best interests of people for whom they have a professional responsibility.

(b) Social workers whose personal problems, psychosocial distress, legal problems, substance abuse, or mental health difficulties interfere with their professional judgment and performance should immediately seek consultation and take appropriate remedial action by seeking professional help, making adjustments in workload, terminating practice, or taking any other steps necessary to protect clients and others.

4.06 Misrepresentation

(a) Social workers should make clear distinctions between statements made and actions engaged in as a private individual and as a representative of the social work profession, a professional social work organization, or the social worker's employing agency.

(b) Social workers who speak on behalf of professional social work organizations should accurately represent the official and authorized positions of the organizations.

(c) Social workers should ensure that their representations to clients, agencies, and the public of professional qualifications, credentials, education, competence, affiliations, services provided, or results to be achieved are accurate. Social workers should claim only those relevant professional credentials they actually possess and take steps to correct any inaccuracies or misrepresentations of their credentials by others.

4.07 Solicitations

(a) Social workers should not engage in uninvited solicitation of potential clients who, because of their circumstances, are vulnerable to undue influence, manipulation, or coercion.

(b) Social workers should not engage in solicitation of testimonial endorsements (including solicitation of consent to use a client's prior statement as a testimonial endorsement) from current clients or from other people who, because of their particular circumstances, are vulnerable to undue influence.

4.08 Acknowledging Credit

(a) Social workers should take responsibility and credit, including authorship credit, only for work they have actually performed and to which they have contributed.

(b) Social workers should honestly acknowledge the work of and the contributions made by others.

5. Social Workers' Ethical Responsibilities to the Social Work Profession

5.01 Integrity of the Profession

(a) Social workers should work towards the maintenance and promotion of high standards of practice.

(b) Social workers should uphold and advance the values, ethics, knowledge, and mission of the profession. Social workers should protect, enhance, and improve the integrity of the profession through appropriate study and research, active discussion, and responsible criticism of the profession.

(c) Social workers should contribute time and professional expertise to activities that promote respect for the value, integrity, and competence of the social work profession. These activities may include teaching, research, consultation, service, legislative testimony, presentations in the community, and participation in their professional organizations.

(d) Social workers should contribute to the knowledge base of social work and share with colleagues their knowledge related to practice, research, and ethics. Social workers should seek to contribute to the profession's literature and to share their knowledge at professional meetings and conferences.

(e) Social workers should act to prevent the unauthorized and unqualified practice of social work.

5.02   Evaluation and Research

(a) Social workers should monitor and evaluate policies, the implementation of programs, and practice interventions.

(b) Social workers should promote and facilitate evaluation and research to contribute to the development of knowledge.

(c) Social workers should critically examine and keep current with emerging knowledge relevant to social work and fully use evaluation and research evidence in their professional practice.

(d) Social workers engaged in evaluation or research should carefully consider possible consequences and should follow guidelines developed for the protection of evaluation and research participants. Appropriate institutional review boards should be consulted.

(e) Social workers engaged in evaluation or research should obtain voluntary and written informed consent from participants, when appropriate, without any implied or actual deprivation or penalty for refusal to participate; without undue inducement to participate; and with due regard for participants' well-being, privacy, and dignity. Informed consent should include information about the nature, extent, and duration of the participation requested and disclosure of the risks and benefits of participation in the research.

(f) When evaluation or research participants are incapable of giving informed consent, social workers should provide an appropriate explanation to the participants, obtain the participants' assent to the extent that they are able, and obtain written consent from an appropriate proxy.

(g) Social workers should never design or conduct evaluation or research that does not use consent procedures, such as certain forms of naturalistic observation and archival research, unless rigorous and responsible review of the research had found it to be justified because of its prospective scientific, educational, or applied value and unless equally effective alternative procedures that do not involve waiver of consent are not feasible.

(h) Social workers should inform participants of their right to withdraw from evaluation and research at any time without penalty.

(i) Social workers should take appropriate steps to ensure that participants in evaluation and research have access to appropriate supportive services.

(j) Social workers engaged in evaluation or research should protect participants from unwarranted physical or mental distress, harm, danger, or deprivation.

(k) Social workers engaged in the evaluation of services should discuss collected information only for professional purposes and only with people professionally concerned with this information.

(l) Social workers engaged in evaluation of research should ensure the anonymity or confidentiality of participants and of the data obtained from them. Social workers should inform participants of any limits of confidentiality, the measures that will be taken to ensure confidentiality, and when any records containing research data will be destroyed.

(m) Social workers who report evaluation and research results should protect participants' confidentiality by omitting identifying information unless proper consent has been obtained authorizing disclosure.

(n) Social workers should report evaluation and research findings accurately. They should not fabricate or falsify results and should take steps to correct any errors later found in published data using standard publication methods.

(o) Social workers engaged in evaluation or research should be alert to and avoid conflicts of interest and dual relationships with participants, should inform participants when a real or potential conflict of interest arises, and should take steps to resolve the issue in a manner that makes participants' interests primary.

(p) Social workers should educate themselves, their students, and their colleagues about responsible research practices.

6. Social Workers' Ethical Responsibilities to the Broader Society

6.01   Social Welfare

Social workers should promote the general welfare of society, from local to global levels, and the development of people, their communities, and their environments. Social workers should advocate for living conditions conducive to the fulfillment of basic human needs and should promote social, economic, political, and cultural values and institutions that are compatible with the realization of social justice.

6.02   Public Participation

Social workers should facilitate informed participation by the public in shaping social policies and institutions.

6.03   Public Emergencies

Social workers should provide appropriate professional services in public emergencies to the greatest extent possible.

6.04   Social and Political Action

(a) Social workers should engage in social and political action that seeks to ensure that all people have equal access to the resources, employment, services, and opportunities they require to meet their basic human needs and to develop fully. Social workers should be aware of the impact of the political arena on practice and should advocate for changes in policy and legislation to improve social conditions in order to meet basic human needs and promote social justice.

(b) Social workers should act to expand choice and opportunity for all people, with special regard for vulnerable, disadvantaged, oppressed, and exploited people and groups.

(c) Social workers should promote conditions that encourage respect for cultural and social diversity within the United States and globally. Social workers should promote policies and practices that demonstrate respect for difference, support the expansion of cultural knowledge and resources, advocate for programs and institutions that demonstrate cultural competence, and promote policies that safeguard the rights of and confirm equity and social justice for all people.

(d) Social workers should act to prevent and eliminate domination of, exploitation of, and discrimination against any person, group, or class on the basis of race, ethnicity, national origin, color, sex, sexual orientation, age, marital status, political belief, religion, or mental or physical disability.

Index